PRENTICE HALL

MIDDLE GRADES
MATH
TOOLS FOR SUCCESS

COURSE 1

Practice Workbook

ISBN 0-13-435419-2

Printed in the United States of America.
9 10 11 12 13 14   04 03 02 01 00

Editorial Services: Visual Education Corporation

PRENTICE HALL

Table of Contents

Answers to Practice Worksheets appear in the Teacher's Edition and in the back of each Chapter Support File.

Practice 1-1 Organizing and Displaying Data

1. Choose a page from a book you are reading. Choose 50 words on that page. Using these 50 words, complete the frequency table.

Letter	Tally	Frequency
t		
s		
r		
n		
d		

2. Make a line plot for your frequency table.

3. Which letter occurred most frequently in your sample? least frequently? _____

Use the line plot at the right to answer Exercises 4–7.

4. What information is displayed in the line plot?
   _____

**Time Spent Doing
Homework Last Night
(min)**

5. How many students spent time doing homework last night?
   _____

6. How many students spent at least a half hour on homework?
   _____

7. What is the range of time spent on homework last night?
   _____

8. A kennel is boarding dogs that weigh the following amounts (in pounds).

5	62	43	48	12	17	29	74
8	15	4	11	15	26	63	

   a. What is the range of the dogs' weights? _____

   b. How many of the dogs weigh under 50 lb? _____

▬▬ Practice 1-2 Problem-Solving Strategy:
Make a Table

Make a table to solve each problem.

1. How many ways are possible to make change for 36¢?

   _____

2. Tom has a $20 bill, a $10 bill, a $5 bill, and a $1 bill. List the total costs possible for items he could buy if he receives no change.

   _____

3. A club began with 4 members. At each meeting every member must bring 2 new people. These new people become members. How many members will there be at the fourth meeting?

   _____

4. Colleen is making raffle tickets for the school's give-away drawing. She wants to use the digits 2, 5, and 7 to make three-digit numbers. How many different three-digit numbers can she make if she uses each digit once?

   _____

Use any strategy to solve each problem. Show all your work.

5. Gavin sells popcorn at basketball games. A large box costs $.75, and a small box costs $.40. One night he sold 45 boxes and collected a total of $25. How many large and how many small boxes of popcorn did Gavin sell?

   _____

6. Find the total number of triangles in the figure. _____

   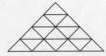

7. How many squares are contained in the floor tile below? _____

8. Find the smallest number that meets all of the following criteria. _____
   - when you divide the number by 5 there are 3 left over
   - when you divide the number by 8 there are 2 left over
   - when you divide the number by 9 there are 4 left over

▬▬Practice 1-3 *Mean, Median, and Mode*

Find the mean, median, and mode for each set of data.

1. 85, 91, 76, 85, 93 _____

2. 72, 76, 73, 74, 75 _____

3. 5, 7, 9, 10, 9, 9, 10, 5 _____

4. 129, 156, 118, 147, 131, 129 _____

5. 86, 87, 95, 96, 88, 94, 98 _____

Use the tables for Exercises 6–11.

6. What is the mean height of the active volcanoes listed? (Find the mean to the nearest foot.)

_____

7. What is the median height of the active volcanoes listed?

_____

8. What is the mode of the heights of the active volcanoes listed?

_____

9. What is the mean of the wages listed?

_____

10. What is the median of the wages listed?

_____

11. What is the mode of the wages listed?

_____

Active Volcanoes

Name	Height Above Sea Level (ft)
Camaroon Mt.	13,354
Mount Erebus	12,450
Asama	8,300
Gerde	9,705
Sarychev	5,115
Ometepe	5,106
Fogo	9,300
Mt. Hood	11,245
Lascar	19,652

Source: *The Universal Almanac*

Hourly Wages of Production Workers 1991 (includes benefits)

Country	Wage
Austria	$17.47
Brazil	$2.55
Finland	$20.57
France	$15.26
Hong Kong	$3.58
Japan	$14.41
Mexico	$2.17
Spain	$12.65
United States	$15.45

Source: *The Universal Almanac*

Each student in a class has taken five tests. The teacher allows the students to pick the mean, median, or mode for each set of scores. Which average should each student pick in order to have the highest average?

12. 100, 87, 81, 23, 19 _____

13. 90, 80, 74, 74, 72 _____

14. 80, 80, 70, 67, 68 _____

15. 75, 78, 77, 70, 70 _____

16. 100, 47, 45, 32, 31 _____

17. 86, 86, 77, 14, 12 _____

18. 79, 78, 77, 76, 85 _____

19. 86, 80, 79, 70, 70 _____

Course 1 Chapter 1

Practice 1-4 Using Spreadsheets to Organize Data

Gervase works after school and on weekends at a pet store, where he is paid $5 per hour. He uses the following spreadsheet to keep track of the time he works and the money he earns.

	A	B	C	D	E
1	Day	Time In (P.M.)	Time Out (P.M.)	Hours Worked	Amount Earned
2	Monday	4	7		
3	Tuesday	4	7		
4	Thursday	4	8		
5	Saturday	1	9		
6			Total		

1. How can the value of cell D2 be calculated?

   _____

2. How can the value of cell E2 be calculated?

   _____

3. Write the formula to find the value of cell D6.

   _____

4. Write the formula to find the value of cell E6.

   _____

5. How many hours does Gervase work in a week?

   _____

6. How much does Gervase earn in a week?

   _____

7. Determine Gervase's weekly earnings if he receives a $1 per hour raise.

   _____

8. Determine Gervase's weekly earnings if he receives a $1 per hour raise and works 4 hours on Friday night.

   _____

9. Rosario worked for $14.50 an hour on the weekdays and $15.25 an hour on the weekends. On Monday she worked 3 hours, on Tuesday she worked 5 hours, and on Saturday and Sunday she worked 8 hours each day.

   a. Make a spreadsheet similar to the one above. Use column B for hourly wage, column C for hours worked, and column D for amount earned.

   b. How much money did Rosario make each day and at the end of one week?

   _____

   _____

■■■ *Practice 1-5* Reading and Understanding Graphs

Use the circle graph for Exercises 1–3.

Major Elements Found in the Body

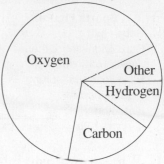

1. Which element is found in the greatest quantity in the body?

   _____

2. What are the three elements named?

   _____

3. Why might there be a portion labeled "other"?

   _____

   _____

Use the bar graph for Exercises 4–6.

4. Which part of the world has the greatest number of operating nuclear reactors?

   _____

5. Which parts of the world have less than 40 nuclear reactors in operation?

   _____

6. Which part of the world has about twice as many nuclear reactors in operation as the Far East?

   _____

Nuclear Reactors in Operation

Number of Reactors (y-axis: 20, 40, 60, 80, 100, 120, 140, 160)

Countries (x-axis): N. America, Central Am., W. Europe, E. Europe, Mid. East, Africa, Far East

Country

Use the line graph for Exercises 7 and 8.

7. What overall trend does the line graph show?

   _____

   _____

8. During which 10-year period did the percent of unmarried men, ages 25–29, decrease?

   _____

Percent of Men Aged 25–29 Who Have Never Married

Number of Men (%) (y-axis: 10, 20, 30, 40, 50)

Year (x-axis: 1960, 1970, 1980, 1990)

Circle A, B, C, or D. Which type of graph—circle, bar, or line—would be most appropriate to display the data?

9. the height of a child from ages 1 to 6

   A. circle graph   **B.** bar graph   **C.** line graph   **D.** any graph

Practice 1-6 Making Bar and Line Graphs

Use the table below to answer Exercises 1–3.

All-Time Favorite Sports Figures

Sports Figure	Number of Votes
Babe Ruth	29
Babe Didrikson Zaharias	22
Jackie Robinson	18
Billie Jean Moffitt King	17
Muhammad Ali	14
Jim Thorpe	13

Source: *The Book of Lists #3, The People's Almanac*

1. What would you label the horizontal axis for a bar graph of the data?

   _____

2. What interval would you use for the vertical axis of the bar graph?

   _____

3. Construct a bar graph displaying the number of votes for all-time favorite sports figures.

Use the table below to answer Exercises 4 and 5.

Daily Use of Petroleum in the U.S.
(millions of barrels)

Year	Number
1950	6.5
1955	8.5
1960	9.8
1965	11.5
1970	14.7
1975	16.3
1980	17.1
1985	15.7
1990	16.9

Source: *U.S. Dept. of Energy, Annual Energy Review*

4. Construct a line graph for the amount of petroleum used daily in the U.S.

5. What overall trend does the line graph show?

   _____

   _____

Practice 1-7 Misleading Graphs

There are only two used car dealers in Auto
City, Junkers and Clunkers. Monthly auto
sales for January, February, and March
are shown for Clunkers.

Clunker's Monthly Auto Sales	
January	15
February	14
March	13

1. Draw a bar graph that Junkers could use to
   show that Clunkers' business is really falling off.

2. Draw a line graph that Clunkers could use to show that
   business has been stable.

3. What is the actual decline in auto sales for Clunkers?
   _____

4. Using data from the first three months of the year, can you
   determine if sales for the whole year will be bad? Explain.

   _____

   _____

   _____

Use the line graph for Exercises 5 and 6.

5. What is wrong with the way the graph is drawn?

   _____

   _____

6. What impression does the graph try
   to present?

   _____

   _____

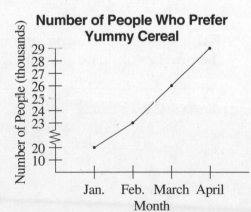

Number of People Who Prefer Yummy Cereal

Practice 2-1 Patterns and Number Sense

Sketch the next two designs in each pattern.

1.

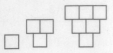

2.

Find the next three terms in each number pattern.

3. 3, 5, 7, 9, _____

4. 34, 31, 28, 25, _____

5. 2, 6, 18, 54, _____

6. 12, 20, 28, 36, _____

7. 54, 53, 52, 51, _____

8. 7, 8, 10, 13, _____

Find the next three terms in each number pattern. Write a rule to describe each number pattern.

9. 4, 7, 10, 13, ▪, ▪, ▪

_____

_____

10. 2, 4, 8, 16, ▪, ▪, ▪

_____

_____

11. 19, 29, 39, 49, ▪, ▪, ▪

_____

_____

12. 8, 11, 14, 17, ▪, ▪, ▪

_____

_____

13. 135, 125, 115, 105, ▪, ▪, ▪

_____

_____

14. 5, 10, 20, 40, ▪, ▪, ▪

_____

_____

15. Write the first five terms in a number pattern starting with the number 6. Write the rule that describes your pattern.

_____

_____

Practice 2-2 Problem-Solving Strategy: Look for a Pattern

Use Look for a Pattern to solve each problem.

1. A radio station held a contest to give away concert tickets. On the first day, the first caller won. On the second day, the second caller won. On the third day, the fourth caller won. On the fourth day, the seventh caller won. Assuming that this pattern continued, did the thirtieth caller ever win?

   _____

2. Three drawings are shown. What would the next three look like?

Use any strategy to solve each problem. Show all your work.

3. Find two numbers with a product of 72 and a sum of 17.

   _____

4. Juana is one year younger than her husband, Leo. The product of their ages is 650. How old is each?

   _____

5. A carpenter charges a basic fee of $25, plus $22 per hour. How much will she charge Ms. Lin if she works for 18 hours?

   _____

6. The product of two numbers is 442. The sum of the two numbers is 43. Find the two numbers.

   _____

7. There are 42 students who signed up for youth camp and 56 students who signed up for family camp. There are 15 students who are signed up for both camps. What is the total number of students who are signed up for camp?

   _____

8. Marquetta charged the Lees a basic fee of $35, plus $25 per hour for repairing their washing machine. What did the Lees pay if it took Marquetta 2.5 hours to finish the job?

   _____

Practice 2-3 The Order of Operations

Which operation would you perform first?

1. $4 + 6 \times 9$

_____

2. $(7 - 5) \times 3$

_____

3. $14 \div 2 \times 3$

_____

4. $18 - 5 + 3$

_____

5. $5 \times 2 + 6$

_____

6. $(9 + 14) - 8 \div 2$

_____

Find the value of the expression.

7. $8 - 3 \times 1 + 5$

_____

8. $(43 - 16) \times 5$

_____

9. $14 \times 6 \div 3$

_____

10. $100 \div (63 - 43)$

_____

11. $9 \times (3 \times 5)$

_____

12. $7 \times (8 + 6)$

_____

13. $15 - (5 + 7)$

_____

14. $(12 - 9) \times (6 + 1)$

_____

15. $(9 - 3) \times 2$

_____

16. $8 - 3 \times 2 + 7$

_____

17. $(9 - 4) \times 6$

_____

18. $35 - 5 \times 3$

_____

Compare. Use <, >, or = to complete each statement.

19. $5 - 3 \times 1 \ \square \ (5 - 3) \times 1$

20. $(4 + 8) \times 3 \ \square \ 4 + 8 \times 3$

21. $3 \times (8 - 2) \ \square \ 3 \times 8 - 2$

22. $(7 + 2) \times 4 \ \square \ 7 + 2 \times 4$

23. $4 + (20 \div 4) \ \square \ (4 + 20) \div 4$

24. $42 - (35 + 4) \ \square \ 42 - 35 + 4$

25. $(9 - 2) \times 3 \ \square \ 9 - 2 \times 3$

26. $55 + 10 - 7 \ \square \ 55 + (10 - 7)$

Place parentheses in each equation to make it true.

27. $6 + 7 \times 4 - 2 = 26$

_____

28. $14 - 5 \div 3 = 3$

_____

29. $27 \div 4 + 5 - 1 = 2$

_____

30. $6 \times 7 + 2 - 1 = 53$

_____

Practice 2-4 Variables and Expressions

Write a variable expression for each model. Squares represent ones. Shaded rectangles represent variables.

1.

_____

2.

_____

3.

_____

Choose a calculator, mental math, or paper and pencil to evaluate each expression.

4. $56 \div b$ for $b = 7$

_____

5. $3m$ for $m = 9$

_____

6. $8n$ for $n = 9$

_____

7. $4y + 6$ for $y = 18$

_____

8. $v + 16$ for $v = 9$

_____

9. $2t - 8$ for $t = 21$

_____

10. $2(4e)$ for $e = 5$

_____

11. $12 - 2g$ for $g = 3$

_____

12. $3pq$ for $p = 3$ and $q = 5$

_____

13. $7n - (m + 18)$ for $n = 4$ and $m = 10$

_____

14. $9r + 16$ for $r = 8$

_____

15. $s(58 + t)$ for $s = 2$ and $t = 7$

_____

16. $24 - 4t$ for $t = 4$

_____

17. $3v + 5k$ for $v = 3$ and $k = 6$

_____

18. $5d - (h + 9)$ for $d = 3$ and $h = 5$

_____

Complete each table by evaluating the expression for the given values of x.

19.

x	$x + 7$
2	9
5	12
8	
11	
	21

20.

x	$5x$
3	
6	
9	
12	
	75

21.

x	$125 - x$
15	
30	
45	
60	
	50

22.

x	$6x + 5$
2	
4	
	41
8	
10	

Practice 2-5 Writing Variable Expressions

Write two word phrases for each variable expression.

1. $5m$

_____
_____
_____

2. $8 + b$

_____
_____
_____

3. $15q$

_____
_____
_____

4. $c - 10$

_____
_____
_____

5. $18 \div a$

_____
_____
_____

6. $27 - m$

_____
_____
_____

7. $v \div 21$

_____
_____
_____

8. $8r$

_____
_____
_____

9. $t + 17$

_____
_____
_____

Choose A, B, C, or D.

10. Which word phrase does *not* describe the expression $24 - x$?

   A. 24 decreased by x **B.** a difference of 24 and x

   C. 24 minus x **D.** 24 less than x

11. Which word phrase does *not* describe the expression $36r$?

   A. 36 times r **B.** the product of 36 and r

   C. 36 added to r **D.** 36 multiplied by r

Write a variable expression for each word phrase.

12. nine less than t

_____

13. eleven more than a number

_____

14. 700 divided by a number

_____

15. two times the number of windows

_____

16. b divided by seven

_____

17. 81 increased by n

_____

18. twelve times the number of muffin pans

_____

19. $15 times the number of hours

_____

20. 8 less than a number

_____

Practice 2-6 Modeling Equations That Use Addition or Subtraction

State whether the number given is a solution to the equation.

1. $m + 7 = 18$; $m = 11$

2. $14 = 9 + v$; $v = 6$

3. $19 = 17 + y$; $y = 3$

4. $w - 17 = 24$; $w = 41$

5. $93 = b - 43$; $b = 146$

6. $53 = m - 14$; $m = 67$

7. $n - 53 = 69$; $n = 122$

8. $78 = b + 19$; $b = 59$

9. $47 + a = 153$; $a = 104$

Choose a calculator, paper and pencil, or mental math to solve each equation.

10. $t + 19 = 47$

11. $v + 14 = 76$

12. $94 = y + 32$

13. $86 = a + 29$

14. $w - 53 = 76$

15. $53 = z - 19$

16. $112 = x - 74$

17. $49 = c + 19$

18. $b + 24 = 52$

19. $117 = 69 + a$

20. $e - 84 = 79$

21. $62 = g - 27$

If possible, write an equation and solve each problem.
If it is not possible to solve, explain why.

22. Some brown eggs and 8 white eggs make a dozen. How many brown eggs are there?

23. Tomás ran 6 mi. How long will it take him to run 10 mi?

24. Zack lost 5 pounds to reach a trim 89 pounds. How heavy had he been?

25. It took Bekka 12 min to walk to school. How long will it take her to walk to the store?

Practice 2-7 Modeling Equations That Use Multiplication or Division

State whether the number given is a solution to the equation.

1. $8c = 80; c = 10$

_____

2. $b \div 7 = 8; b = 56$

_____

3. $9m = 108; m = 12$

_____

4. $y \div 9 = 17; y = 163$

_____

5. $9r = 72; r = 7$

_____

6. $14b = 56; b = 4$

_____

7. $48 = y \div 4; y = 12$

_____

8. $32 = y \div 8; y = 256$

_____

9. $17a = 41; a = 3$

_____

10. $w \div 21 = 17; w = 357$

_____

11. $21c = 189; c = 8$

_____

12. $52 = y \div 6; y = 302$

_____

Choose a calculator, paper and pencil, or mental math to solve each equation.

13. $905 = 5a$

_____

14. $6v = 792$

_____

15. $12 = y \div 12$

_____

16. $b \div 18 = 21$

_____

17. $80 = 16b$

_____

18. $19m = 266$

_____

19. $d \div 1,000 = 10$

_____

20. $g \div 52 = 18$

_____

21. $672 = 21f$

_____

22. $z \div 27 = 63$

_____

23. $43h = 817$

_____

24. $58 = j \div 71$

_____

Solve.

25. Lea drove 420 mi and used 20 gal of gas. How many miles per gallon did her car get? _____

26. Ty spent $15.00 on folders that cost $3.00 each. How many folders did he buy?

_____

27. Bob pays a $2.00 toll each way when going to and from work. How much does he pay in four weeks, working five days a week? _____

28. Julia wants to buy copies of a book to give as presents. How many books can she buy if they are on sale for $12 each, and she has $100 to spend? _____

■■■ *Practice 3-1* *Exploring Decimal Models*

Draw a model for each decimal.

1. 0.4

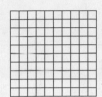

2. 0.72

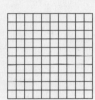

3. 0.10

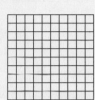

Write each decimal in words.

4. 0.9

_____

5. 0.1

_____

6. 0.04

_____

7. 0.07

_____

8. 0.29

_____

9. 0.46

_____

10. 0.80

_____

11. 0.30

_____

12. 0.03

_____

Write a decimal for each model.

13.

_____

14.

_____

15.

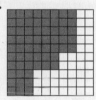

_____

Write a decimal for the given words.

16. three tenths

_____

17. fifty-two hundredths

_____

18. eight tenths

_____

19. two hundredths

_____

20. seventy-nine hundredths

_____

21. forty hundredths

_____

How many hundredths are equivalent to each amount?

22. five tenths

_____

23. nine tenths

_____

24. one tenth

_____

25. How many tenths are equivalent to 30 hundredths?

_____

Practice 3-2 Reading and Writing Whole Numbers and Decimals

Write each number in words.

1. 1,760

2. 84,508

3. 75,398,012

_____

_____

_____

Write each number in standard form.

4. three thousand forty

_____

5. eleven billion

_____

6. one hundred ten

_____

7. 400,000 + 20,000 + 8,000 + 400 + 6

_____

8. 921 million, 750 thousand, 33

_____

9. eighty-two thousand sixty

_____

What is the value of the digit 7 in each number?

10. 0.7

_____

11. 4.00712

_____

12. 2.179

_____

13. 28,467.089

_____

14. 348.92971

_____

15. 72.14

_____

Write each number in words.

16. 12.873

_____

17. 8.0552

_____

18. 0.00065

_____

Write each number in standard form.

19. six and five thousandths

_____

20. nine hundred fifty-four ten thousandths

_____

21. 20 + 0.01 + 0.003 + 0.0008

_____

22. 30 + 4 + 0.9 + 0.02

_____

23. forty and eight hundredths

_____

24. 200 + 10 + 0.04

_____

▰▰▰*Practice 3-3* Comparing and Ordering Decimals

Use >, <, or = to complete each statement.

1. 0.62 ☐ 0.618   **2.** 9.8 ☐ 9.80   **3.** 1.006 ☐ 1.02   **4.** 41.3 ☐ 41.03

5. 2.01 ☐ 2.011   **6.** 1.400 ☐ 1.40   **7.** 5.079 ☐ 5.08   **8.** 12.96 ☐ 12.967

9. 15.8 ☐ 15.800   **10.** 7.98 ☐ 7.89   **11.** 8.02 ☐ 8.020   **12.** 5.693 ☐ 5.299

Graph each set of numbers on a number line.

13. 0.2, 0.6, 0.5   **14.** 0.26, 0.3, 0.5, 0.59, 0.7

15. Circle A, B, C, or D. Three points are graphed on the number line below. Read statements A–D. Which statement is true?

A. 0.3 < 0.5 and 0.7 < 0.5   **B.** 0.5 > 0.3 and 0.7 < 0.5

C. 0.3 < 0.7 and 0.7 > 0.5   **D.** 0.7 < 0.5 and 0.3 < 0.5

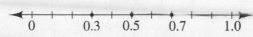

16. Draw a number line. Use 10 tick marks. Label the first tick 0.6 and the tenth tick 0.7. Graph 0.67 and 0.675.

a. Which is greater, 0.67 or 0.675? _____

b. How does the number line show which number is greater?

_____

17. Models for three decimals are shown below.

a. Write the decimal that each model represents.

_____

b. Order the decimals from least to greatest.

_____

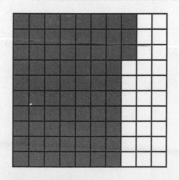

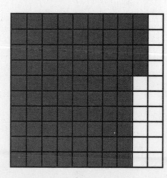

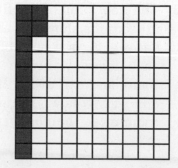

Practice 3-4 Problem-Solving Strategy: Guess and Test

Use *guess and test* to solve each problem.

1. A deli sells ham sandwiches for $2 and roast beef sandwiches for $3. A committee organizing a family reunion placed orders for 85 sandwiches. The bill came to $218, before tax. How many ham sandwiches were ordered?

   _____

2. Tickets for a community dinner cost $4 for adults and $3 for children. A total of 390 tickets was sold, earning $1,380. How many of each type of ticket were sold?

   _____

3. Place the digits 3, 4, 7, 9, and 12 in the circles at the right so that the product is the same left to right and up and down. What is the product?

   _____

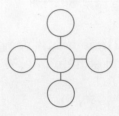

Use any strategy to solve each problem. Show your work.

4. Two numbers have a sum of 42 and a product of 432. What are the two numbers? _____

5. Two numbers have a sum of 70 and a product of 1,189. What are the numbers? _____

6. Louise, Bill, and Fran each had a different piece of fruit packed in their lunches. An apple, an orange, and a banana were packed. Louise won't eat apples. Bill is allergic to oranges. Fran eats only bananas. What piece of fruit did each person have?

   _____

   _____

7. Paco joins a baseball card club. He brings 2 cards to the first meeting, 3 cards to the second meeting, 5 cards to the third meeting, and 8 cards to the fourth meeting. If he continues this pattern, how many cards will he bring to the fifth meeting?

   _____

8. The floor plan of the first floor of a museum is shown at the right. If you enter at A, is it possible to go through each doorway only one time, see each room, and exit at B? If this can be done, show how. You may enter each room more than one time.

   _____

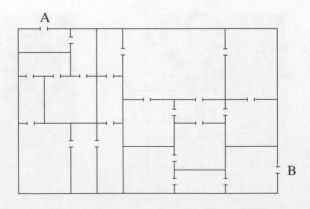

Practice 3-5 Modeling the Addition and Subtraction of Decimals

Write the sum or difference shown by the models.

1. 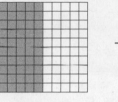 +

_____ + _____ = _____

2.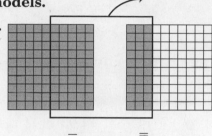

_____ − _____ = _____

Add or subtract. Use models as needed.

3.	4.	5.	6.
3.9 + 2.6	7.1 − 0.8	0.26 + 0.53	0.54 − 0.21

7.	8.	9.	10.
1.2 + 0.91	3.92 + 0.63	1.52 − 0.27	0.93 − 0.57

11.	12.	13.	14.
1.2 + 4.9	0.83 − 0.24	4.1 + 5.7	0.81 + 0.56

15.	16.	17.	18.
0.26 − 0.07	0.9 + 0.8	2.07 − 1.48	1.59 + 2.41

19. $0.96 - 0.47$

_____

20. $0.27 + 0.85$

_____

21. $1.96 - 0.97$

_____

22. $0.52 + 0.78$

_____

23. $2.3 - 0.54$

_____

24. $4.5 + 0.72$

_____

25. $6.37 - 2.59$

_____

26. $4 - 1.80$

_____

27. $3.56 + 4.70$

_____

Practice 3-6 Rounding and Estimating Data

Round to the place of the underlined digit.

1. 1.1<u>0</u>9   **2.** 2.3<u>5</u>7   **3.** 4.87<u>7</u>2   **4.** 5.8<u>0</u>45

_____   _____   _____   _____

Use rounding or front-end estimation. Estimate each sum or difference.

5. $8.92   **6.** $32.18   **7.** $29.99   **8.** $26.49
    + 5.19   − 14.09   + 15.29   − 13.99

9. $21.95   **10.** $83.49   **11.** $1.87   **12.** $43.87
    − 7.15   − 56.13   + 5.28   + 26.15

13. $15.49   **14.** $23.57   **15.** $49.17   **16.** $19.95
   + 12.86   − 18.99   − 5.88   + 21.36

Use front-end estimation to estimate each total cost.

17. $2.59 + $3.76 + $2.41 _____   **18.** $8.19 + $2.46 + $3.57 _____

19. $3.61 + $2.17 + $5.84 _____   **20.** $9.14 + $8.72 + $5.63 _____

Circle A, B, C, or D. Choose the sum that is most appropriate for the given range of low and high estimates.

21. low: 11; high: 14   **22.** low: 24; high: 25

    A. 2.89 + 3.51 + 6.62   **A.** 9.83 + 8.16 + 7.58
    B. 1.27 + 1.89 + 2.34   **B.** 7.08 + 8.91 + 9.23
    C. 3.45 + 4.62 + 7.32   **C.** 8.12 + 7.43 + 6.27
    D. 2.01 + 3.22 + 4.56   **D.** 10.06 + 6.94 + 8.58

23. low: 56; high: 58   **24.** low: 52; high: 54

    A. 14.78 + 23.92 + 16.37   **A** 14.78 + 21.05 + 14.71
    B. 34.96 + 2.43 + 8.74   **B.** 23.86 + 15.93 + 18.92
    C. 16.88 + 17.12 + 25.94   **C.** 15.96 + 18.72 + 19.41
    D. 15.78 + 23.41 + 18.50   **D.** 42.56 + 8.32 + 5.64

25. Dom has $13. He wants to buy 2 audio cassette tapes that cost $5.79 each and a notebook that costs $1.89. Does Dom have enough money? Explain your estimation strategy.

_____

_____

Practice 3-7 Adding and Subtracting Decimals

First estimate. Then find the sum or difference.

1. $0.6 + 5.8$ 　　**2.** $2.1 + 3.4$ 　　**3.** $3.4 - 0.972$ 　　**4.** $3.1 - 2.076$

_____ 　　_____ 　　_____ 　　_____

5. $8.13 - 2.716$ 　　**6.** $5.91 + 2.38$ 　　**7.** $3.086 + 6.152$ 　　**8.** $4.7 - 1.9$

_____ 　　_____ 　　_____ 　　_____

9. $9.3 - 3.9$ 　　**10.** $5.2 - 1.86$ 　　**11.** $15.98 + 26.37$ 　　**12.** $9.27 + 15.006$

_____ 　　_____ 　　_____ 　　_____

13. $5.9 \quad 2.803$ 　　**14.** $15.7 - 8.923$ 　　**15.** $4.19 - 2.016$ 　　**16.** $14.75 - 6.9264$

_____ 　　_____ 　　_____ 　　_____

17. $5.1 + 4.83 + 9.002$ 　　**18.** $3 + 4.02 + 8.6$ 　　**19.** $4.7 + 5.26 + 8.931$

_____ 　　　　_____ 　　　　_____

Solve each equation.

20. $x - 0.31 = 6.29$ 　　**21.** $b + 16.12 = 18.57$ 　　**22.** $28.854 = 3.722 + y$

_____ 　　　　_____ 　　　　_____

23. $14.56 = 5.51 + s$ 　　**24.** $t - 0.785 = 2.49$ 　　**25.** $y + 4.027 = 5.954$

_____ 　　　　_____ 　　　　_____

26. $47.809 = m + 34.731$ 　　**27.** $p - 23.509 = 56.84$ 　　**28.** $67.357 = n - 43.516$

_____ 　　　　_____ 　　　　_____

Use the table at the right for Exercises 29–31.

29. Find the sum of the decimals given in the chart. What is the meaning of this sum?

_____

_____

Ages of Workers Earning Hourly Pay

Age of Workers	Part of Work Force
16–19	0.08
20–24	0.15
25–34	0.29
35–44	0.24
45–54	0.14
55–64	0.08
65 & over	0.02

Source: *Bureau of Labor Statistics, U.S. Dept. of Labor*

30. What part of the hourly work force is ages 25–44? _____

31. Which three age groups combined represent about one-fourth of the hourly work force?

_____

_____

Practice 3-8 Metric Units of Length

Find each length in millimeters and centimeters.

1. _____

   ___ mm, ___ cm

2. _____

   _____

3. _____

   _____

4. _____

   _____

Find the perimeter of each figure.

5. _____

6. _____

7. _____

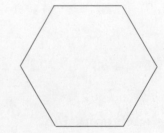

8. Draw a figure that has a perimeter of 14 cm.

Is each measurement reasonable? If not, choose a reasonable measurement. Circle A, B, C, or D.

9. Your friend is 1,500 mm tall.

   A. 1.5 mm   **B.** 1,500 cm

   C. 1.5 km   **D.** reasonable

10. Your desk is about 50 mm wide.

   A. 50 m   **B.** 50 cm

   C. 5 m   **D.** reasonable

11. A tree is about 20 km tall.

   A. 20 m   **B.** 2 km

   C. 20 cm   **D.** reasonable

12. An envelope is about 24 cm long.

   A. 2.4 cm   **B.** 24 mm

   C. 2.4 m   **D.** reasonable

Circle A, B, C, or D. What unit would you use to measure each item?

13. the height of an office building

   A. km   **B.** m

   C. cm   **D.** mm

14. the width of a page of a text

   A. km   **B.** m

   C. cm   **D.** mm

15. the length of an ant

   A. km   **B.** m

   C. cm   **D.** mm

16. the depth of a lake

   A. km   **B.** m

   C. cm   **D.** mm

Practice 3-9 Metric Units of Mass and Capacity

Choose an appropriate metric unit of mass for each.

1. a grain of rice

_____

2. a bag of groceries

_____

3. a feather

_____

4. a cat

_____

5. a leaf

_____

6. an eraser

_____

Choose an appropriate metric unit of capacity for each.

7. a gasoline tank

_____

8. a coffee mug

_____

9. 6 raindrops

_____

10. a pitcher of juice

_____

11. a swimming pool

_____

12. a can of paint

_____

State whether each of the following is best measured in terms of mass or capacity.

13. a bag of potatoes

_____

14. water in a birdbath

_____

15. an apple

_____

16. a box of raisins

_____

17. a cup of hot cider

_____

18. the inside of a
refrigerator

_____

19. juice in a
baby's bottle

_____

20. water in a
fish tank

_____

21. water in a
watering can

_____

Write *true* or *false*.

22. The mass of the horse is about 500 kg.

_____

23. Jean drank 5.8 L of juice at breakfast.

_____

24. A mug holds 250 mL of hot chocolate.

_____

25. A penny is about 3 kg.

_____

26. A teaspoon holds about 5 L.

_____

27. A textbook is about 1 kg.

_____

Practice 3-10 Measuring Elapsed Time

Clark is trying to plan his Saturday. He estimates each activity will take the following times.

Make a schedule for Clark's day if he wakes up at 7:00 A.M. Assume all his activities are done in the given order.

	Activity	Amount of Time	Time of Day
1.	Get up, eat breakfast	30 min	7:00 A.M. - 7:30 A.M.
2.	Mow lawn	1 h	
3.	Rake yard	2 h	
4.	Wash, wax car	45 min	
5.	Walk dog	15 min	
6.	Clean room	45 min	
7.	Eat lunch	30 min	
8.	Shop for school clothes	1 h 30 min	
9.	Read book	45 min	
10.	Do homework	1 h 15 min	
11.	Baby-sit brother	2 h	
12.	Eat supper	45 min	
13.	Get ready for party	30 min	
14.	Ride to party	20 min	
15.	Party	2 h	
16.	Ride home	20 min	

Find the elapsed time between each pair of times.

17. 2:12 P.M. and 10:18 P.M.

18. 9:35 A.M. and 8:48 P.M.

19. 6:45 P.M. and 11:24 A.M.

20. 2:55 A.M. and 8:13 A.M.

21. 7:00 P.M. and 8:56 P.M.

22. 8:22 P.M. and 11:47 A.M.

Solve.

23. The movie begins at 7:45 P.M. and lets out at 10:20 P.M. How long is the movie?

Practice 4-3 The Distributive Property

Find the areas of the two parts of each rectangle. Then find the total area of the rectangle.

1.
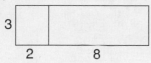
3
2   8

_____

2.
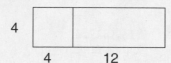
4
4   12

_____

3.
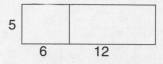
5
6   12

_____

Write the missing numbers.

4. $8 \times (9 + 4) = (\boxed{} \times 9) + (8 \times \boxed{})$

5. $(4 \times 7) + (4 \times 5) = 4 \times (\boxed{} + 5)$

6. $9 \times (7 - 1) = (9 \times \boxed{}) - (\boxed{} \times 1)$

7. $(5 \times 7) + (5 \times 6) = \boxed{} \times (7 + 6)$

8. $3 \times (7 + 9) = (\boxed{} \times 7) + (3 \times \boxed{})$

9. $8 \times (9 - 6) = (8 \times \boxed{}) - (\boxed{} \times 6)$

Use the distributive property to rewrite and simplify.

10. 7×53

11. 8×97

12. 5×402

_____ _____ _____

_____ _____ _____

13. 8×103

14. 9×213

15. 7×49

_____ _____ _____

_____ _____ _____

Simplify.

16. $9 \times (5 + 3) \times 4 - 6$

17. $(8 + 7) \times 3 \times 2$

18. $5 \times 7 \times 3 + (5 - 4)$

_____ _____ _____

19. $6 \times (8 - 3) + 9 \times 4$

20. $7 \times (8 - 2) \times 4 + 9$

21. $(8 + 6) \times 3 \times 9$

_____ _____ _____

Insert parentheses into each equation so that a true statement is formed.

22. $8 + 6 \div 2 + 9 - 3 \times 2 = 19$

23. $6 \times 3 + 4 - 9 + 7 = 26$

_____ _____

24. $9 - 4 \times 6 - 8 + 1 = 21$

25. $8 + 7 \div 5 + 2 + 7 \times 3 = 30$

_____ _____

Practice 4-4 Using Models to Multiply Decimals

Write a multiplication sentence to describe the model.

1.

2.

3.

_____   _____   _____

4.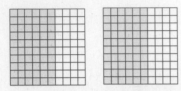

5.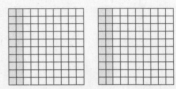

_____   _____

Draw a model to find each product.

6. 0.4×0.4 _____

7. 0.6×0.9 _____

8. 0.8×0.7 _____

9. 3×0.5 _____

10. 2×0.9 _____

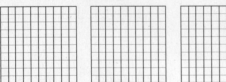 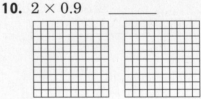

Write a multiplication sentence you could use to model each situation.

11. A pen costs $.59. How much would a dozen pens cost?

   _____

12. A mint costs $.02. How much would a roll of 10 mints cost?

   _____

13. A bottle of juice has a deposit of $.10 on the bottle. How much deposit would there be on 8 bottles? _____

14. An orange costs $.09. How much would 2 dozen oranges cost?

   _____

Practice 4-5 Multiplying Decimals

Place a decimal point in each product.

1. $4.3 \times 2.9 = 1247$ **2.** $0.279 \times 53 = 14787$ **3.** $4.09 \times 3.96 = 161964$

_____   _____   _____

4. $5.90 \times 6.3 = 3717$ **5.** $0.74 \times 83 = 6142$ **6.** $2.06 \times 15.9 = 32754$

_____   _____   _____

Find each product mentally.

7. 8.7×100 **8.** 43.59×0.1 **9.** 5.97×10

_____   _____   _____

10. 246×0.01 **11.** 726×0.1 **12.** 5.23×100

_____   _____   _____

Find each product.

13.	14.	15.	16.
5.342	0.19	6.4	240
$\times\ 13$	$\times\ 0.05$	$\times\ 0.09$	$\times\ 0.02$

17.	18.	19.	20.
43.79	0.72	6.72	0.27
$\times\ 42$	$\times\ 0.43$	$\times\ 83$	$\times\ 8.1$

21.	22.	23.	24.
5.96	421	9.87	1.09
$\times\ 0.08$	$\times\ 0.07$	$\times\ 5.6$	$\times\ 2.14$

25.	26.	27.	28.
8.76	42.7	4.03	0.25
$\times\ 29$	$\times\ 8.9$	$\times\ 0.09$	$\times\ 0.78$

Write a digit in each space so that a true multiplication problem results. Place a decimal point in each product. No digit may be repeated. Use digits 2 to 9 in each problem.

29.

```
    1 □ . □
  ×   □ . □
  ─────────
  4 □ □ □
```

30.

```
    1 □ . □
  ×   □ . □
  ─────────
  □ □ 5 □
```

■ Practice 4-6 Using Models to Divide Decimals

Complete each sentence.

1.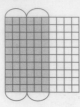

$\boxed{} \div 0.3 = 2$

2.

$0.4 \div 0.04 = \boxed{}$

3.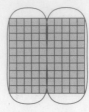

$1 \div \boxed{} = 2$

4.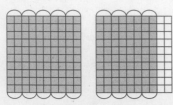

$\boxed{} \div 0.2 = 9$

5.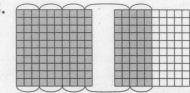

$1.5 \div \boxed{} = 5$

Draw a model to find each quotient.

6. $0.4 \div 0.08$ _____

7. $0.8 \div 0.4$ _____

8. $0.9 \div 0.15$ _____

9. $1.5 \div 0.75$ _____

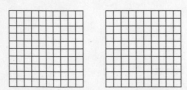

10. $1.2 \div 0.12$ _____

Practice 4-7 *Dividing Decimals by Whole Numbers*

Find each quotient.

1. $1.8 \div 6$

2. $16\overline{)3.2}$

3. $17\overline{)5.1}$

4. $9\overline{)21.6}$

5. $15\overline{)123}$

6. $108 \div 5$

7. $50\overline{)17.5}$

8. $24\overline{)120.60}$

9. $19\overline{)11.4}$

10. $14\overline{)889}$

11. $5\overline{)316}$

12. $4.15 \div 5$

13. $7.8 \div 10$

14. $89.1 \div 100$

15. $10\overline{)46.3}$

16. $0.6 \div 10$

17. $20\overline{)23.4}$

18. $5\overline{)0.18}$

19. $26.12 \div 4$

20. $7.3 \div 5$

21. $0.12 \div 8$

22. $6\overline{)3.39}$

23. $1.45 \div 10$

24. $20\overline{)12.6}$

**Choose a calculator, pencil and paper, or mental math
to solve.**

25. A package of 25 mechanical pencils costs $5.75. How much does
each pencil cost? _____ _____

26. A sales clerk is placing books side by side on a shelf. She has 12
copies of the same book. If the books cover 27.6 in. of the shelf,
how thick is each book? _____

27. A car traveled 234.3 mi on 11 gal of gas. How many miles per
gallon did the car average? _____

28. Mr. Garza spent $80.73 on 9 cassette tapes. If they all cost the
same amount, how much did each cassette tape cost?

_____ _____

Practice 4-8 Dividing Decimals by Decimals

Find each quotient.

1. $0.4 \div 0.02$ **2.** $3.9 \div 0.05$ **3.** $0.2\overline{)26}$ **4.** $2.05 \div .05$

_____   _____   _____   _____

5. $0.4\overline{)1.08}$ **6.** $0.68 \div 0.2$ **7.** $0.7\overline{)3.57}$ **8.** $0.6\overline{)5.88}$

_____   _____   _____   _____

9. $0.02\overline{)0.06}$ **10.** $0.09\overline{)0.108}$ **11.** $0.04\overline{)0.024}$ **12.** $0.07\overline{)0.3304}$

_____   _____   _____   _____

13. $11.18 \div 4.3$ **14.** $5.7\overline{)24.225}$ **15.** $3.6\overline{)18.072}$ **16.** $7.1\overline{)63.19}$

_____   _____   _____   _____

17. $5.2\overline{)43.68}$ **18.** $9.3\overline{)49.29}$ **19.** $65.026 \div 8.2$ **20.** $14.82 \div 5.7$

_____   _____   _____   _____

21. $5.3\overline{)2.279}$ **22.** $9.1\overline{)6.552}$ **23.** $4.042 \div 8.6$ **24.** $2.9\overline{)2.175}$

_____   _____   _____   _____

Choose a calculator, paper and pencil, or mental math to divide.

25. $2.4 \div 0.08$ **26.** $9.6 \div 0.6$ **27.** $0.21 \div 0.003$ **28.** $3.2 \div 0.04$

_____   _____   _____   _____

29. $0.49 \div 0.7$ **30.** $3.6 \div 0.06$ **31.** $0.9 \div 0.003$ **32.** $5.25 \div 0.01$

_____   _____   _____   _____

33. $0.75 \div 0.15$ **34.** $4.56 \div 0.02$ **35.** $7.11 \div 0.01$ **36.** $1.45 \div 0.05$

_____   _____   _____   _____

■ Practice 4-9 Problem-Solving Strategy: Too Much or Too Little Information

Solve if possible. If not, tell what information is needed.

1. The electrician charged Audun for a wiring job. The rates were $48 per hour plus $23.56 for parts. What was the total amount Audun was charged?

   _____

2. A horse measured 12.6 hands in height. If a hand is about 4 in., what was the horse's height in inches?

   _____

3. Camilla worked 8 hours a week for 14 weeks. She earns $4.55 per hour. How much did she earn?

   _____

4. Kosey's school sold 397 tickets for a fun night and collected $893.25. If expenses came to $247.93, how much profit did the school make?

   _____

5. The Picnic Committee split up posters to be distributed to local merchants. If each committee member took 12 posters, how many merchants can display a poster about the picnic?

   _____

6. Rashida bought some boxes of greeting cards. One type cost $5.98 a box. Another type cost $7.29 a box. Rashida bought 15 boxes, and spent $97.56 total. How many boxes of each type did she buy?

   _____

7. Herman plans to work for 30 weeks. He will earn $175 per week. He plans to save all except $55 per week so that he can pay back a loan of $1,000. How much will he save in 16 weeks?

   _____

8. Jodi has some quarters and dimes. How many possible amounts of money could she have?

   _____

   _____

▰▰▰ *Practice 4-10* Patterns of Changing Metric Units

Change each measure to meters.

1. 800 mm   **2.** 50 cm   **3.** 2.6 km   **4.** 7 km   **5.** 250 mm

_____   _____   _____   _____   _____

6. 35 km   **7.** 40 mm   **8.** 300 cm   **9.** 1.8 km   **10.** 450 cm

_____   _____   _____   _____   _____

Change each measure to liters.

11. 160 mL   **12.** 0.36 kL   **13.** 0.002 kL   **14.** 240.9 mL   **15.** 368.5 mL

_____   _____   _____   _____   _____

16. 8 kL   **17.** 80 mL   **18.** 17.3 mL   **19.** 0.09 kL   **20.** 330 mL

_____   _____   _____   _____   _____

Change each measure to grams.

21. 4,000 mg   **22.** 7 kg   **23.** 56,000 mg   **24.** 0.19 kg   **25.** 754.8 mg

_____   _____   _____   _____   _____

26. 600 mg   **27.** 90 kg   **28.** 2,800 mg   **29.** 0.4 kg   **30.** 58.1 mg

_____   _____   _____   _____   _____

Use mental math to complete each statement.

31. ■ km = 3,400 cm   **32.** 42,000 mL = ■ kL   **33.** 3.7 cm = ■ km

_____   _____   _____

34. 5,100 mL = ■ L   **35.** 77.8 mm = ■ cm   **36.** 9.5 kL = ■ mL

_____   _____   _____

37. 2.564 mL = ■ kL   **38.** ■ km = 400,000 mm   **39.** 948 mm = ■ cm

_____   _____   _____

40. ■ mL = 0.648 kL   **41.** ■ kg = 6,000 mg   **42.** ■ mL = 0.1678 kL

_____   _____   _____

Practice 5-1 Mental Math and Divisibility

Use mental math to determine whether the first number is divisible by the second.

1. 475; 5 _____　　**2.** 5,296; 3 _____　　**3.** 843; 2 _____　　**4.** 76,780; 10 _____

5. 456,790; 5 _____　　**6.** 3,460; 2 _____　　**7.** 4,197; 3 _____　　**8.** 100,005; 10 _____

Use mental math to determine whether the number is divisible by 1, 2, 3, 5, 9, or 10.

9. 126　　　　**10.** 257　　　　**11.** 430　　　　**12.** 535

_____　　_____　　_____　　_____

13. 745　　　　**14.** 896　　　　**15.** 729　　　　**16.** 945

_____　　_____　　_____　　_____

17. 4,580　　　　**18.** 6,331　　　　**19.** 7,952　　　　**20.** 8,000

_____　　_____　　_____　　_____

21. 19,450　　　　**22.** 21,789　　　　**23.** 43,785　　　　**24.** 28,751

_____　　_____　　_____　　_____

Find the digit to make each number divisible by 9.

25. 54,78☐　　　　**26.** 42,☐97　　　　**27.** 83,2☐4　　　　**28.** 53☐,904

Circle A, B, C, or D. Which number satisfies the given conditions?

29. divisible by 1, 3, and 5

A. 10　　　　**B.** 93　　　　**C.** 45　　　　**D.** 54

30. divisible by 1, 2, 3, and 9

A. 18　　　　**B.** 9　　　　**C.** 6　　　　**D.** 60

31. divisible by 1, 2, 5, and 10

A. 406　　　　**B.** 400　　　　**C.** 205　　　　**D.** 716

32. divisible by 1, 2, 3, 5, and 10

A. 708　　　　**B.** 65　　　　**C.** 200　　　　**D.** 600

33. There are 159 students to be grouped into relay teams. Each team is to have the same number of students. Can each team have 3, 5, or 6 students?

_____

Practice 5-2 Using Models and Factor Trees

1. The diagram below shows the different rectangles that can be formed using exactly 24 square tiles. Use the diagram to determine all the factors of 24.

_____

Tell whether each number is prime or composite.

2. 53   **3.** 86   **4.** 95   **5.** 17

_____   _____   _____   _____

6. 24   **7.** 27   **8.** 31   **9.** 51

_____   _____   _____   _____

10. 103   **11.** 47   **12.** 93   **13.** 56

_____   _____   _____   _____

Complete each factor tree.

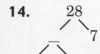

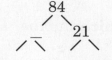
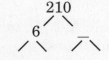

Find the prime factorization of each number using a factor tree.

18. 58   **19.** 72   **20.** 40   **21.** 30

_____   _____   _____   _____

22. 120   **23.** 100   **24.** 144   **25.** 310

_____   _____   _____   _____

Find the number with the given prime factorization.

26. $2 \times 2 \times 5 \times 7 \times 11$ **27.** $2 \times 3 \times 5 \times 7 \times 11$

_____   _____

28. $2 \times 2 \times 13 \times 17$ **29.** $7 \times 11 \times 13 \times 17$

_____   _____

Practice 5-3 Greatest Common Factor

Make a list to find the GCF of each set of numbers.

1. 8, 12   **2.** 18, 27   **3.** 15, 23   **4.** 17, 34

_____   _____   _____   _____

5. 24, 12   **6.** 18, 24   **7.** 5, 25   **8.** 20, 25

_____   _____   _____   _____

9. 10, 15   **10.** 25, 75   **11.** 14, 21   **12.** 18, 57

_____   _____   _____   _____

13. 32, 24, 40   **14.** 25, 60, 75   **15.** 12, 35, 15   **16.** 15, 35, 20

_____   _____   _____   _____

Use prime factorization to find the GCF of each set of numbers.

17. 28, 24   **18.** 27, 36   **19.** 15, 305   **20.** 24, 45

_____   _____   _____   _____

21. 57, 27   **22.** 24, 48   **23.** 56, 35   **24.** 29, 87

_____   _____   _____   _____

25. 75, 200   **26.** 90, 160   **27.** 72, 108   **28.** 50, 96

_____   _____   _____   _____

29. 8, 42, 60   **30.** 75, 90, 120   **31.** 45, 70, 120   **32.** 200, 450, 300

_____   _____   _____   _____

Solve.

33. The GCF of two numbers is 850. Neither number is divisible by the other. What is the smallest that these two numbers could be?

_____

34. The GCF of two numbers is 479. One number is even and the other number is odd. Neither number is divisible by the other. What is the smallest that these two numbers could be?

_____

35. The GCF of two numbers is 871. Both numbers are even and neither is divisible by the other. What is the smallest that these two numbers could be?

_____

Practice 5-4 Using Fraction Models

Name the fraction modeled.

1. _____

2. _____

3. _____

4. _____

5. _____

6. _____

7. _____

8. _____

9. _____

10. _____

11. _____

12. _____

Model each fraction.

13. $\frac{1}{12}$

14. $\frac{5}{12}$

15. $\frac{11}{12}$

16. $\frac{2}{6}$

17. $\frac{4}{6}$

18. $\frac{1}{6}$

19. $\frac{7}{10}$

20. $\frac{9}{10}$

21. $\frac{5}{10}$

22. $\frac{3}{5}$

23. $\frac{2}{5}$

24. $\frac{4}{5}$

Round each fraction to the nearest half-unit.

25.

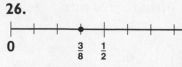

_____

26.

_____

27.

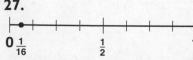

_____

Practice 5-5 Equivalent Fractions

Name the fractions modeled. Tell whether they are equivalent.

1.

2.

3.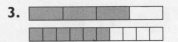

_____   _____   _____

By what number can you multiply the numerator and denominator of the first fraction to get the second fraction?

4. $\frac{2}{3}, \frac{4}{6}$ _____

5. $\frac{3}{8}, \frac{15}{40}$ _____

6. $\frac{7}{10}, \frac{42}{60}$ _____

7. $\frac{3}{4}, \frac{9}{12}$ _____

By what number can you divide the numerator and denominator of the first fraction to get the second fraction?

8. $\frac{6}{8}, \frac{3}{4}$ _____

9. $\frac{70}{80}, \frac{7}{8}$ _____

10. $\frac{15}{60}, \frac{1}{4}$ _____

11. $\frac{75}{100}, \frac{3}{4}$ _____

Write two fractions equivalent to each fraction.

12. $\frac{3}{10}$ _____

13. $\frac{7}{8}$ _____

14. $\frac{5}{6}$ _____

15. $\frac{3}{4}$ _____

16. $\frac{15}{20}$ _____

17. $\frac{8}{12}$ _____

18. $\frac{15}{45}$ _____

19. $\frac{8}{32}$ _____

State whether each fraction is in simplest form. If not, write it in simplest form.

20. $\frac{15}{35}$ _____

21. $\frac{22}{55}$ _____

22. $\frac{11}{15}$ _____

23. $\frac{25}{32}$ _____

24. $\frac{34}{36}$ _____

25. $\frac{19}{57}$ _____

26. $\frac{20}{53}$ _____

27. $\frac{125}{200}$ _____

28. $\frac{27}{54}$ _____

29. $\frac{30}{41}$ _____

30. $\frac{9}{17}$ _____

31. $\frac{85}{110}$ _____

32. Use the numbers 2, 5, 8, and 20 to write two pairs of equivalent fractions.

_____

Practice 5-6 Mixed Numbers and Improper Fractions

Circle A, B, C, or D. Find the mixed number that represents the amount.

1.

   A. $2\frac{1}{4}$ **B.** $1\frac{3}{4}$ **C.** $2\frac{3}{4}$ **D.** $3\frac{3}{4}$

2.

   A. $4\frac{5}{6}$ **B.** $3\frac{5}{6}$ **C.** $2\frac{5}{6}$ **D.** $3\frac{1}{6}$

3.

   A. $4\frac{5}{8}$ **B.** $4\frac{3}{8}$ **C.** $5\frac{5}{8}$ **D.** $5\frac{3}{8}$

4.

   A. $5\frac{3}{5}$ **B.** $4\frac{2}{5}$ **C.** $6\frac{2}{5}$ **D.** $5\frac{2}{5}$

Write each improper fraction as a mixed number.

5. $\frac{15}{2}$ _____   6. $\frac{8}{3}$ _____   7. $\frac{5}{2}$ _____   8. $\frac{7}{3}$ _____

9. $\frac{11}{10}$ _____   10. $\frac{7}{6}$ _____   11. $\frac{9}{8}$ _____   12. $\frac{11}{8}$ _____

13. $\frac{15}{8}$ _____   14. $\frac{21}{4}$ _____   15. $\frac{17}{3}$ _____   16. $\frac{17}{4}$ _____

17. $\frac{17}{5}$ _____   18. $\frac{17}{6}$ _____   19. $\frac{21}{10}$ _____   20. $\frac{25}{4}$ _____

Write each whole or mixed number as an improper fraction.

21. $1\frac{7}{8}$ _____   22. $2\frac{3}{4}$ _____   23. $7\frac{1}{3}$ _____   24. 8 _____

25. $3\frac{3}{4}$ _____   26. 4 _____   27. $5\frac{5}{6}$ _____   28. $1\frac{9}{10}$ _____

29. $2\frac{3}{8}$ _____   30. $4\frac{7}{8}$ _____   31. $2\frac{3}{5}$ _____   32. 6 _____

33. $3\frac{11}{12}$ _____   34. $2\frac{7}{12}$ _____   35. $5\frac{4}{15}$ _____   36. $2\frac{7}{15}$ _____

▬▬ *Practice 5-7* Least Common Multiple

Find the LCM of each set of numbers. Use lists of multiples of each number.

1. 5, 10   **2.** 2, 3   **3.** 6, 8   **4.** 4, 6

_____ _____ _____ _____

5. 8, 10   **6.** 5, 6   **7.** 12, 15   **8.** 8, 12

_____ _____ _____ _____

9. 9, 15   **10.** 6, 15   **11.** 6, 9   **12.** 6, 18

_____ _____ _____ _____

13. 3, 5   **14.** 4, 5   **15.** 9, 21   **16.** 7, 28

_____ _____ _____ _____

17. 4, 6, 8   **18.** 6, 8, 12   **19.** 4, 9, 12   **20.** 6, 9, 12

_____ _____ _____ _____

21. 6, 12, 15   **22.** 8, 12, 15

_____ _____

Find the LCM of each set of numbers. Use prime factorization.

23. 18, 21   **24.** 15, 21   **25.** 18, 24   **26.** 21, 24

_____ _____ _____ _____

27. 15, 30   **28.** 24, 30   **29.** 24, 72   **30.** 18, 72

_____ _____ _____ _____

31. 8, 42   **32.** 16, 42   **33.** 8, 56   **34.** 6, 81

_____ _____ _____ _____

35. 8, 30   **36.** 16, 30   **37.** 18, 30   **38.** 45, 60

_____ _____ _____ _____

39. 12, 24, 16   **40.** 8, 16, 20   **41.** 12, 16, 20   **42.** 15, 20, 25

_____ _____ _____ _____

43. At one store hot dogs come in packages of eight. Hot dog buns come in packages of twelve. What is the least number of packages of each type that you can buy and have no hot dogs or buns left over?

_____

Practice 5-8 Comparing and Ordering Fractions

Compare using $<$, $>$, or $=$.

1. $2\frac{14}{17}$ ☐ $1\frac{16}{17}$ 2. $\frac{15}{21}$ ☐ $\frac{5}{7}$ 3. $2\frac{7}{8}$ ☐ $2\frac{5}{6}$ 4. $1\frac{1}{2}$ ☐ $2\frac{1}{3}$

5. $3\frac{15}{16}$ ☐ $3\frac{21}{32}$ 6. $4\frac{7}{8}$ ☐ $3\frac{9}{10}$ 7. $5\frac{9}{10}$ ☐ $5\frac{18}{20}$ 8. $4\frac{7}{8}$ ☐ $5\frac{1}{8}$

9. $1\frac{19}{20}$ ☐ $2\frac{1}{20}$ 10. $4\frac{5}{6}$ ☐ $5\frac{19}{20}$ 11. $7\frac{3}{10}$ ☐ $7\frac{9}{30}$ 12. $2\frac{7}{15}$ ☐ $1\frac{14}{15}$

13. $4\frac{19}{24}$ ☐ $4\frac{7}{12}$ 14. $5\frac{19}{20}$ ☐ $6\frac{21}{22}$ 15. $4\frac{15}{20}$ ☐ $4\frac{21}{28}$ 16. $1\frac{2}{16}$ ☐ $1\frac{1}{4}$

Order each set of fractions from least to greatest.

17. $\frac{9}{10}, \frac{5}{6}, \frac{14}{15}$

18. $1\frac{7}{8}, 1\frac{7}{12}, 1\frac{5}{6}$

19. $\frac{14}{15}, \frac{9}{10}, \frac{11}{12}$

_____   _____   _____

20. $2\frac{1}{4}, 3\frac{7}{8}, 3\frac{5}{6}$

21. $\frac{2}{3}, \frac{4}{5}, \frac{7}{30}, \frac{11}{15}$

22. $2\frac{1}{6}, 1\frac{3}{4}, 3\frac{7}{8}, 2\frac{1}{10}$

_____   _____   _____

23. $\frac{5}{12}, \frac{17}{30}, \frac{3}{5}$

24. $1\frac{5}{6}, 2\frac{1}{6}, 1\frac{11}{12}, 1\frac{11}{18}$

25. $\frac{17}{20}, 1\frac{18}{25}, 2\frac{31}{36}$

_____   _____   _____

Circle A, B, C, or D.

26. Which fraction is greater than $\frac{31}{36}$?   27. Which fraction is less than $\frac{8}{15}$?

    A. $\frac{2}{3}$ **B.** $\frac{7}{8}$ **A.** $\frac{4}{7}$ **B.** $\frac{3}{5}$

    C. $\frac{1}{2}$ **D.** $\frac{13}{24}$ **C.** $\frac{17}{30}$ **D.** $\frac{4}{9}$

28. Explain how you could answer Exercise 27 without finding
common denominators or using a calculator.

_____

_____

▰▰▰ *Practice 5-9* *Fractions and Decimals*

Write the decimal represented by each model. Write this decimal as a fraction in simplest form.

1.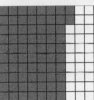

2.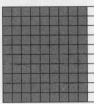

3.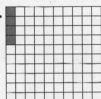

_____ _____ _____

Write each decimal as a fraction or mixed number in simplest form.

4. 0.6 ____   **5.** 1.25 ____   **6.** 0.74 ____   **7.** 0.29 ____

8. 0.635 ____   **9.** 0.8 ____   **10.** 6.16 ____   **11.** 0.95 ____

12. 0.645 ____   **13.** 0.782 ____   **14.** 0.493 ____   **15.** 0.758 ____

Write each fraction or mixed number as a decimal. Use a bar to show a repeating decimal.

16. $\frac{5}{6}$ ____   **17.** $\frac{7}{8}$ ____   **18.** $\frac{9}{16}$ ____   **19.** $2\frac{4}{25}$ ____

20. $\frac{1}{12}$ ____   **21.** $1\frac{4}{15}$ ____   **22.** $\frac{9}{100}$ ____   **23.** $\frac{8}{9}$ ____

24. $\frac{7}{25}$ ____   **25.** $\frac{3}{50}$ ____   **26.** $\frac{1}{125}$ ____   **27.** $\frac{6}{11}$ ____

Circle A, B, C, or D. Which shows the numbers in order from least to greatest?

28. $\frac{1}{2}$, 0.75, $\frac{5}{8}$, 0.9, $\frac{7}{10}$

    A. $\frac{1}{2}$, $\frac{5}{8}$, 0.75, $\frac{7}{10}$, 0.9   **B.** $\frac{1}{2}$, $\frac{5}{8}$, $\frac{7}{10}$, 0.75, 0.9

    C. 0.9, 0.75, $\frac{7}{10}$, $\frac{5}{8}$, $\frac{1}{2}$ **D.** $\frac{1}{2}$, 0.75, $\frac{5}{8}$, $\frac{7}{10}$, 0.9

29. 0.875, $\frac{9}{10}$, $\frac{15}{16}$, 0.98

    A. 0.98, $\frac{15}{16}$, $\frac{9}{10}$, 0.875   **B.** $\frac{15}{16}$, $\frac{9}{10}$, 0.875, 0.98

    C. $\frac{9}{10}$, 0.875, $\frac{15}{16}$, 0.98   **D.** 0.875, $\frac{9}{10}$, $\frac{15}{16}$, 0.98

Practice 5-10 Problem-Solving Strategy: Work Backward

Work backward to solve.

1. At the end of a board game, Al had 57 game dollars. During the game he had won $200, lost $150, won $25, lost $10, and lost $35. How much money did Al have at the start?

   _____

2. Jan spent half of the money she had on a coat. She spent half of what remained on a dress. Next, she spent half of what remained on a pair of boots. She returned home with $57. How much money did Jan have before shopping?

   _____

3. Bill gathered some eggs on Monday. On Tuesday, he gathered half as many eggs, plus an egg, as what he gathered on Monday. On Wednesday, he gathered half the difference of the number of eggs he gathered on Monday and Tuesday, plus an egg. If he gathered 5 eggs on Wednesday, how many eggs did Bill gather on Monday?

   _____

4. Carli spent a third of her money, and then spent $4 more. She then spent half of what money remained. It cost her $1 for the bus ride home. She then had $5 left. How much money did she start with?

   _____

5. Mick picked a number, doubled it, added 8, divided by 4, and had a result of 12. What number did Mick pick?

   _____

6. It takes Jenni 50 minutes to get ready for school. The drive to school takes 15 minutes. She needs 8 minutes to get to her locker, then to her first class. If school begins at 8:30 A.M., what is the latest Jenni should get up in the morning?

   _____

7. On May 31, Hayden's uncle and grandfather came to visit him. Hayden's grandfather visits every three days, and his uncle visits every twelve days. What is the first day in May that both visited Hayden on the same day?

   _____

Practice 6-1 Estimating Sums and Differences

Write the fraction shown by each model. Then round to the nearest $\frac{1}{2}$.

1. [model] _____

2. [model] _____

Estimate each sum or difference.

3. $\frac{5}{16} + \frac{5}{8}$ _____

4. $\frac{10}{12} + \frac{4}{5}$ _____

5. $\frac{8}{10} - \frac{1}{2}$ _____

6. $4\frac{1}{4} - 1\frac{7}{9}$ _____

7. $8\frac{6}{8} - 2\frac{1}{3}$ _____

8. $2\frac{2}{5} - \frac{5}{6}$ _____

9. $\frac{3}{4} + \frac{3}{8}$ _____

10. $\frac{7}{10} - \frac{1}{6}$ _____

11. $5\frac{7}{8} + 3\frac{3}{4}$ _____

12. $8\frac{1}{12} - 3\frac{9}{10}$ _____

13. $6\frac{5}{7} - 2\frac{2}{9}$ _____

14. $3\frac{5}{8} + 2\frac{3}{10}$ _____

15. Name three fractions that round to $\frac{1}{2}$.

_____

16. Name three fractions that round to 1.

_____

17. The fabric for the play costumes costs $5.95/yd. Patti needs $2\frac{7}{8}$ yd for one costume and $3\frac{5}{8}$ yd for another one. About how much will she spend on these costumes?

_____

18. One bag of oranges costs $2.99 and weighs about $3\frac{7}{8}$ lb. Individual oranges are sold at $.89/lb. Which is the better buy? Explain.

_____

_____

_____

Practice 6-2 Modeling Like Denominators

Write an addition sentence for each model.

1.

2.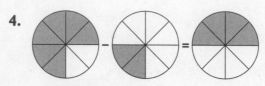

_____

_____

Write a subtraction sentence for each model.

3. 

4.

_____

_____

Find each sum or difference. Write each answer in simplest form.

5. $\frac{1}{4} + \frac{2}{4}$ _____

6. $\frac{7}{10} - \frac{4}{10}$ _____

7. $\frac{5}{8} - \frac{3}{8}$ _____

8. $\frac{1}{8} + \frac{5}{8}$ _____

9. $\frac{5}{8} + \frac{2}{8}$ _____

10. $\frac{3}{10} + \frac{6}{10}$ _____

11. $\frac{11}{12} - \frac{5}{12}$ _____

12. $\frac{11}{16} - \frac{3}{16}$ _____

13. $\frac{3}{6} + \frac{1}{6}$ _____

14. $\frac{7}{9} - \frac{3}{9}$ _____

15. What is the total amount of sugar the recipe at the right calls for?

_____

16. Martha decides to double the recipe. How much brown sugar will she use?

_____

Martha's Cookie Recipe
1 cup shortening
2 eggs
$\frac{1}{4}$ cup white sugar
$\frac{1}{4}$ cup brown sugar
$1\frac{1}{2}$ cup flour
1 teaspoon vanilla

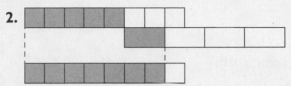 Practice 6-3 *Unlike Denominators*

Write a number sentence for each model.

1.

2.

_____   _____

Find each sum or difference. Use equivalent fractions.

3. $\frac{1}{4} + \frac{2}{3}$ _____

4. $\frac{2}{5} - \frac{1}{10}$ _____

5. $\frac{1}{6} + \frac{1}{4}$ _____

6. $\frac{5}{8} + \frac{1}{4}$ _____

7. $\frac{7}{8} - \frac{1}{2}$ _____

8. $\frac{3}{10} + \frac{4}{5}$ _____

9. $\frac{5}{6} - \frac{2}{5}$ _____

10. $\frac{5}{12} - \frac{1}{4}$ _____

11. $\frac{7}{16} + \frac{1}{8}$ _____

12. $\frac{11}{16} + \frac{5}{8}$ _____

Use estimation to decide if the answer is greater or less than 1. Write > or <. Then add or subtract.

13. $\frac{2}{7} + \frac{1}{2}$ _____

14. $\frac{4}{5} - \frac{3}{4}$ _____

15. $\frac{2}{3} - \frac{1}{6}$ _____

16. $\frac{5}{8} + \frac{2}{3}$ _____

17. $\frac{5}{7} - \frac{1}{5}$ _____

18. $\frac{3}{5} + \frac{7}{10}$ _____

Find x. Write the answer in simplest form.

19. $x + \frac{1}{3} = \frac{5}{6}$ _____

20. $x + \frac{1}{3} = \frac{4}{5}$ _____

21. $x + \frac{2}{5} = \frac{11}{12}$ _____

22. $x + \frac{5}{8} = \frac{11}{12}$ _____

23. Jeanie has a $\frac{3}{4}$-yd piece of ribbon. She needs one $\frac{3}{8}$-yd piece and one $\frac{1}{2}$-yd piece. Can she cut the piece of ribbon into the two smaller pieces? Explain. Draw a model for the problem.

_____

_____

Practice 6-4 Adding Mixed Numbers

Complete to rename each mixed number.

1. $3\frac{9}{8} = 4\frac{\blacksquare}{8}$ _____

2. $5\frac{7}{4} = 6\frac{\blacksquare}{4}$ _____

3. $2\frac{17}{12} = 3\frac{\blacksquare}{12}$ _____

Find each sum.

4. $4\frac{3}{10} + 5\frac{2}{5}$ _____

5. $3\frac{7}{8} + 2\frac{1}{2}$ _____

6. $5\frac{2}{3} + 3\frac{1}{4}$ _____

7. $6\frac{3}{4} + 2\frac{1}{2}$ _____

8. $1\frac{1}{12} + 3\frac{1}{6}$ _____

9. $9\frac{2}{5} + 10\frac{3}{10}$ _____

10. $7\frac{1}{3} + 5\frac{11}{12}$ _____

11. $11\frac{7}{10} + 4$ _____

12. $2\frac{2}{3} + 4\frac{3}{4}$ _____

13. $7\frac{3}{4} + 2\frac{7}{8}$ _____

14. $4\frac{1}{2} + 3\frac{5}{6}$ _____

15. $7\frac{2}{3} + 1\frac{5}{6}$ _____

16. $2\frac{1}{4} + 4\frac{3}{5}$ _____

17. $5\frac{3}{8} + 7\frac{1}{4}$ _____

18. $14\frac{5}{16} + 8\frac{3}{8}$ _____

Solve each equation for x.

19. $x - \frac{11}{12} = 4\frac{5}{12}$

_____

20. $27\frac{2}{5} = x - 3\frac{4}{5}$

_____

21. $x - 7\frac{1}{6} = 9\frac{7}{12}$

_____

22. $22\frac{1}{4} = x - 3\frac{3}{5}$

_____

23. $x - 39\frac{1}{8} = 6\frac{3}{4}$

_____

24. $x - 14\frac{1}{16} = 3\frac{7}{8}$

_____

25. $18\frac{1}{2} = x - 12\frac{1}{6}$

_____

26. $80\frac{1}{10} = x - 5\frac{3}{5}$

_____

27. $x - 9\frac{3}{8} = 2\frac{1}{4}$

_____

28. Estimate the length of rope needed to go around a triangle with sides $6\frac{1}{2}$ ft, $7\frac{3}{4}$ ft, and $10\frac{1}{4}$ ft. _____

Practice 6-5 Subtracting Mixed Numbers

Find the difference.

1. $10\frac{11}{16} - 3\frac{7}{8}$ _____

2. $8\frac{1}{3} - 2\frac{3}{8}$ _____

3. $9 - 3\frac{2}{5}$ _____

4. $5\frac{3}{16} - 2\frac{3}{8}$ _____

5. $8\frac{1}{6} - 3\frac{2}{5}$ _____

6. $7\frac{1}{2} - 3$ _____

7. $2\frac{3}{4} - 1\frac{1}{8}$ _____

8. $4\frac{1}{8} - 2\frac{1}{16}$ _____

9. $9\frac{2}{3} - 3\frac{5}{6}$ _____

10. $2\frac{1}{10} - 1\frac{2}{5}$ _____

11. $15\frac{7}{12} - 8\frac{1}{2}$ _____

12. $6\frac{7}{16} - 2\frac{7}{8}$ _____

13. $27\frac{1}{4}$ $13\frac{11}{12}$ _____

14. $5\frac{2}{5} - 1\frac{1}{4}$ _____

15. $10\frac{2}{3} - 7\frac{3}{4}$ _____

Solve each equation for x.

16. $x + 2\frac{1}{2} = 5\frac{3}{4}$

17. $10\frac{1}{3} + x = 16\frac{5}{12}$

18. $x + 9\frac{1}{16} = 23\frac{7}{8}$

_____

_____

_____

19. $32\frac{1}{5} + x - 35\frac{1}{2}$

20. $x + 17\frac{3}{4} = 25\frac{1}{3}$

21. $27\frac{1}{10} + x = 33\frac{1}{2}$

_____

_____

_____

22. $18\frac{5}{6} + x = 24\frac{3}{8}$

23. $x + 8\frac{3}{16} = 12\frac{3}{8}$

24. $5\frac{1}{2} + x = 9\frac{1}{4}$

_____

_____

_____

Solve.

25. Robbie needs to buy fencing for his square vegetable garden that measures $16\frac{3}{4}$ ft on a side. One side borders the back of the garage. The fencing costs \$4/ft. Estimate how much the fencing for the vegetable garden will cost. _____

26. Paula has 2 yd of elastic. One project needs a piece $\frac{3}{4}$ yd. Does she have enough for another project that needs $1\frac{1}{3}$ yd? Explain.

_____

_____

27. Use a ruler or measuring tape to find the perimeter of your desk. Measure to the nearest half inch.

width:_____   length:_____   perimeter:_____

Practice 6-6 Problem-Solving Strategy: Draw a Diagram

Frank is laying square tiles on a rectangular floor. He wants the perimeter tiles to be a different color for two rows around the edges of the room. The dimensions of the room are 20 ft by 10 ft. Each tile is 1 ft on a side.

1. Draw a diagram to show how Frank could tile the floor. Use two colors.

2. How many border tiles does he need? _____

3. How many inside tiles does he need? _____

Draw a diagram to solve.

4. Jessica is hanging five posters on a 19-ft wall. Each poster is 2 ft wide, and she wants to have 1 ft of space between the posters and an equal amount of space at both ends. Draw a diagram to show the placement of the posters.

5. Suppose you are hanging posters along a 35-ft wall in the hallway. Each poster is 2 ft wide.

   a. What is the greatest number of posters that you could fit along the wall without overlap? _____

   b. What is the greatest number of posters that you could fit along the wall if you kept 2 ft between them? Draw a diagram to show your answer.

Choose any strategy to solve.

6. Matthew earns $.10 for each local newspaper he delivers twice a week. His brother earns $.25 for delivering each Sunday newspaper. They deliver papers to the same number of houses and together they earn $13.95/wk. How many papers does each boy deliver each week?

   _____

7. Megan's car averaged 336 mi on 12 gal of gas. How many gallons of gas did Megan use to drive 1,344 mi on vacation?

   _____

Name _____ Class _____ Date _____

Practice 6-7 *Modeling the Multiplication of Fractions*

Draw a model to represent each product.

1. $\frac{1}{6}$ of $\frac{3}{4}$ **2.** $\frac{2}{5}$ of $\frac{1}{2}$

Find each product.

3. $\frac{3}{5}$ of 10 _____   **4.** $\frac{1}{4}$ of 12 _____   **5.** $\frac{2}{3}$ of 6 _____

6. $\frac{4}{5}$ of $\frac{5}{8}$ _____   **7.** $\frac{5}{6}$ of $\frac{3}{8}$ _____   **8.** $\frac{3}{5}$ of $\frac{1}{2}$ _____

9. $\frac{3}{4}$ of 12 _____   **10.** $\frac{2}{5}$ of 15 _____   **11.** $\frac{3}{16}$ of 8 _____

12. $\frac{1}{2} \times \frac{5}{6}$ _____   **13.** $\frac{3}{4} \times \frac{7}{8}$ _____   **14.** $\frac{1}{3}$ of $\frac{2}{5}$ _____

15. $\frac{3}{5}$ of $\frac{3}{4}$ _____   **16.** $\frac{1}{2} \times \frac{1}{3}$ _____   **17.** $\frac{1}{8} \times \frac{3}{4}$ _____

18. $\frac{2}{5} \times \frac{7}{11}$ _____   **19.** $\frac{2}{3}$ of $\frac{1}{4}$ _____   **20.** $\frac{2}{5} \times \frac{1}{2}$ _____

21. $\frac{1}{4}$ of $\frac{4}{5}$ _____   **22.** $\frac{5}{6} \times \frac{2}{5}$ _____   **23.** $\frac{2}{7}$ of $\frac{3}{5}$ _____

24. $\frac{1}{3}$ of $\frac{9}{10}$ _____   **25.** $\frac{1}{12} \times \frac{3}{4}$ _____   **26.** $\frac{3}{10} \times \frac{3}{5}$ _____

27. Circle A, B, C, or D. Which product does the model represent?

  A. $\frac{1}{4} \times \frac{2}{3}$ **B.** $\frac{3}{4} \times \frac{1}{12}$

  C. $\frac{2}{3} \times \frac{1}{2}$ **D.** $\frac{1}{4} \times \frac{1}{2}$

Practice 6-8 Multiplying Mixed Numbers

Estimate each product.

1. $2\frac{5}{6} \times 1\frac{3}{4}$ _____

2. $3\frac{3}{8} \times 7\frac{1}{4}$ _____

3. $5\frac{3}{8} \times 2\frac{7}{8}$ _____

4. $2\frac{3}{8} \times 4\frac{4}{5}$ _____

5. $6\frac{7}{12} \times 5\frac{9}{10}$ _____

6. $7\frac{1}{3} \times 10\frac{11}{12}$ _____

7. $12\frac{1}{4} \times 3\frac{3}{4}$ _____

8. $8\frac{1}{6} \times 2\frac{1}{4}$ _____

9. $15\frac{2}{3} \times 5\frac{5}{7}$ _____

Find each product.

10. $2\frac{5}{6} \times 1\frac{3}{4}$ _____

11. $3\frac{3}{8} \times 7\frac{1}{4}$ _____

12. $5\frac{3}{8} \times 2\frac{7}{8}$ _____

13. $2\frac{3}{8} \times 4\frac{4}{5}$ _____

14. $6\frac{7}{12} \times 5\frac{9}{10}$ _____

15. $7\frac{1}{3} \times 10\frac{11}{12}$ _____

16. $12\frac{1}{4} \times 3\frac{3}{4}$ _____

17. $8\frac{1}{6} \times 2\frac{1}{4}$ _____

18. $15\frac{2}{3} \times 5\frac{5}{7}$ _____

19. $\frac{1}{4} \times 5\frac{2}{5}$ _____

20. $2\frac{3}{8} \times \frac{4}{5}$ _____

21. $1\frac{1}{2} \times 5\frac{1}{3}$ _____

22. $3\frac{3}{8} \times 6$ _____

23. $\frac{3}{4} \times 1\frac{3}{5}$ _____

24. $9\frac{3}{5} \times \frac{1}{3}$ _____

25. $1\frac{1}{4} \times 2\frac{2}{3}$ _____

26. $1\frac{3}{5} \times \frac{1}{4}$ _____

27. $6\frac{1}{4} \times 1\frac{2}{5}$ _____

28. $\frac{7}{8} \times 3\frac{1}{5}$ _____

29. $5\frac{1}{3} \times 2\frac{1}{4}$ _____

30. $\frac{3}{5} \times 4\frac{1}{2}$ _____

31. $\frac{5}{8} \times 7\frac{3}{5}$ _____

32. $5\frac{1}{3} \times \frac{5}{8}$ _____

33. $2\frac{4}{5} \times \frac{3}{7}$ _____

34. $3\frac{1}{3} \times 3\frac{3}{10}$ _____

35. $5\frac{1}{2} \times \frac{2}{5}$ _____

36. $1\frac{2}{3} \times 3\frac{3}{4}$ _____

37. Ken used a piece of lumber to build a bookshelf. If he made three shelves that are each $2\frac{1}{2}$ ft long, how long was the piece of lumber? _____

38. Deanna's cake recipe needs to be doubled for a party. How much of each ingredient should Deanna use?

Delicious Cake	
flour $2\frac{1}{4}$ c	_____
sugar $1\frac{3}{4}$ c	_____
butter $1\frac{1}{2}$ c	_____
milk $\frac{3}{4}$ c	_____

Practice 6-9 Dividing Fractions and Mixed Numbers

Write the reciprocal of each number.

1. $\frac{7}{10}$ _____   **2.** 4 _____   **3.** $5\frac{1}{3}$ _____   **4.** $\frac{1}{12}$ _____

5. Draw a diagram to show how many $\frac{3}{4}$-ft pieces of string can be cut from a piece of string $4\frac{1}{2}$ ft long.

Divide. Write each answer in simplest form.

6. $\frac{3}{10} \div \frac{4}{5}$ _____   **7.** $\frac{3}{8} \div 3$ _____   **8.** $3 \div 1\frac{4}{5}$ _____

9. $2\frac{1}{5} \div 1\frac{5}{6}$ _____   **10.** $1\frac{1}{2} \div \frac{3}{16}$ _____   **11.** $\frac{1}{4} \div \frac{1}{8}$ _____

12. $1\frac{7}{8} \div \frac{5}{8}$ _____   **13.** $1\frac{3}{4} \div \frac{1}{16}$ _____   **14.** $3 \div \frac{3}{8}$ _____

15. How many $\frac{3}{4}$-c servings are there in a 6-c package of rice?

_____

16. George cut 5 oranges into quarters. How many pieces of orange did he have? _____

Anna bought a package of ribbon 10 yd long. She needs $1\frac{1}{3}$-yd pieces for a bulletin board.

17. How many pieces can Anna cut from the ribbon?

_____

18. Anna decides to use $\frac{2}{3}$-yd pieces. How many pieces can she cut? _____

19. A bulletin board is 56 in. wide and 36 in. high. How many $3\frac{1}{2}$-in. columns can be created?

_____

20. Study the tangram pieces at the right. If the entire square is 1, find the fractional value of each piece. You can cut the tangram pieces to compare them.

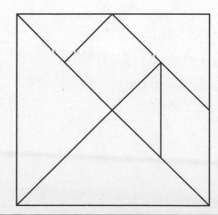

Practice 6-10 Changing Units in the Customary System

Complete each statement.

1. $7\frac{1}{2}$ ft = _____ yd

2. 45 in. = _____ ft

3. $1\frac{1}{4}$ mi = _____ ft

4. $2\frac{1}{2}$ lb = _____ oz

5. 28 fl oz = _____ c

6. $2\frac{3}{4}$ t = _____ lb

7. 3 lb = _____ oz

8. 10 pt = _____ qt

Compare using <, >, or =.

9. $4\frac{1}{3}$ ft ☐ 50 in.

10. 136 oz ☐ $8\frac{1}{2}$ lb

11. 26 fl oz ☐ 3 c

12. 5 qt ☐ $1\frac{1}{4}$ gal

13. 8 yd ☐ 21 ft

14. 4,500 lb ☐ $3\frac{1}{2}$ t

Solve.

15. The odometer of an automobile shows tenths of a mile. How many feet are in $\frac{1}{10}$ mi? _____

16. How many inches are in one mile? _____

17. Jarel bought 3 containers of cottage cheese, each weighing 24 oz. How many pounds did she buy? _____

18. Katie poured 12 oz of juice from a full 6-qt container. How many cups were left in the container? _____

19. The food committee for the end-of-the-year class picnic plans to serve 4-oz hamburger patties. How many pounds of meat should be bought to make 125 hamburgers? _____

Add or subtract. Rename when necessary.

20. 8 ft 3 in.
   $-$ 3 ft 5 in.

21. 12 qt 1 pt
   $+$ 11 qt 1 pt

22. 9 yd 15 in.
   $+$ 7 yd 28 in.

23. 105 lb 8 oz
   $-$ 98 lb 12 oz

24. 3 c 7 fl oz
   $+$ 4 c 6 fl oz

25. 13 yd 2 ft
   $-$ 6 yd 1 ft

Practice 7-1 Exploring Ratios

Write a ratio in three ways to compare each.

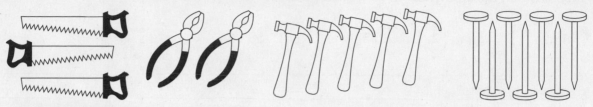

1. saws to pliers

_____

2. hammers to nails

_____

3. saws to nails

_____

4. nails to saws

_____

5. hammers to pliers

_____

6. pliers to saws

_____

7. pliers to nails

_____

8. saws to hammers

_____

9. nails to hammers

_____

Draw a picture to represent each ratio.

10. 7 baseballs : 1 bat

11. 3 CDs to 8 books

12. $\dfrac{2 \text{ c blueberries}}{3 \text{ c cream}}$

13. In Tanya's family, 6 out of 15 people have blue eyes. What is the ratio of those who have blue eyes to those who do not? _____

14. In Fred's class, 8 of the 21 students earned a grade of B or better. What is the ratio of students who did not earn at least a B to those who did? _____

15. In Todd's class, 14 of the students own cats and 9 of the students own dogs. What is the ratio of dog owners to cat owners? _____

16. In Markita's class, there are 15 boys and 12 girls. Write the ratio that represents the number of girls to the number of boys.

_____

Practice 7-2 Equal Ratios and Unit Rates

Write three ratios equal to the given ratio.

1. $8 : 24$ **2.** 15 to 25   **3.** $18 : 36$ **4.** $\frac{12}{15}$

_____   _____   _____   _____

_____   _____   _____   _____

Find the value that makes the ratios equal.

5. $\frac{7}{8} = \frac{\blacksquare}{32}$ **6.** $\frac{5}{4} = \frac{15}{\blacksquare}$ **7.** 8 to 12 = $\blacksquare$ to 6   **8.** $9 : 12 = 3 : \blacksquare$

_____   _____   _____   _____

Write each ratio as a fraction in simplest form.

9. pencils : squares   **10.** flowers : pencils   **11.** pencils : flowers   **12.** pencils : circles

_____   _____   _____   _____

13. squares : flowers   **14.** flowers : squares   **15.** squares : pencils   **16.** circles : flowers

_____   _____   _____   _____

Find the unit rate for each situation.

17. 20 mi in 2 h   **18.** 20 dogs in 10 kennels   **19.** 450 mi in 5 d

_____   _____   _____

20. $60 for 5 books   **21.** 315 grapes for 15 children   **22.** 20 dimes for 4 children

_____   _____   _____

Circle A, B, or C. For each exercise, choose the expression that represents the greatest number.

23. **A.** $\frac{9}{27}$ **B.** $\frac{8}{12}$ **C.** $\frac{2}{2}$ **24.** **A.** $\frac{4}{6}$ **B.** $\frac{7}{14}$ **C.** $\frac{5}{15}$ **25.** **A.** $\frac{10}{16}$ **B.** $\frac{28}{32}$ **C.** $\frac{15}{40}$

26. **A.** $\frac{24}{32}$ **B.** $\frac{12}{18}$ **C.** $\frac{14}{16}$ **27.** **A.** $\frac{30}{45}$ **B.** $\frac{20}{32}$ **C.** $\frac{27}{30}$ **28.** **A.** $\frac{14}{42}$ **B.** $\frac{15}{20}$ **C.** $\frac{16}{24}$

▰▰ *Practice 7-3* Solving Proportions

Does each pair of ratios form a proportion?

1. $\frac{8}{9}, \frac{4}{3}$ **2.** $\frac{20}{16}, \frac{18}{15}$ **3.** $\frac{18}{12}, \frac{21}{14}$ **4.** $\frac{21}{27}, \frac{35}{45}$

5. $\frac{18}{22}, \frac{45}{55}$ **6.** $\frac{38}{52}, \frac{57}{80}$ **7.** $\frac{10}{65}, \frac{18}{87}$ **8.** $\frac{51}{48}, \frac{68}{64}$

Choose a calculator, paper and pencil, or mental math. Find the value of each variable.

9. $\frac{4}{5} = \frac{x}{15}$ **10.** $\frac{8}{m} = \frac{4}{15}$ **11.** $\frac{39}{27} = \frac{26}{m}$ **12.** $\frac{y}{5} = \frac{32}{20}$

13. $\frac{14}{b} = \frac{8}{12}$ **14.** $\frac{a}{18} = \frac{16}{24}$ **15.** $\frac{d}{25} = \frac{12}{15}$ **16.** $\frac{28}{42} = \frac{26}{x}$

17. $\frac{16}{24} = \frac{y}{27}$ **18.** $\frac{50}{8} = \frac{x}{25}$ **19.** $\frac{9}{10} = \frac{c}{45}$ **20.** $\frac{x}{90} = \frac{45}{50}$

Solve each problem.

21. In the 1991–92 National Basketball Association Championship games, the Chicago Bulls won 2 games for each game that the Portland Trailblazers won. If Portland won 2 games, how many did Chicago win? _____
Source: *World Almanac and Book of Facts*

22. In 1915, there was one divorce for every 1,000 people in the United States. If a certain town had a population of 56,000 people, how many divorces would you have expected in that town? _____
Source: *World Almanac and Book of Facts*

23. For every 100 families with TV sets, about 12 families like *Star Trek, the Next Generation.* In a town of 23,400 families who all have TV sets, how many families would you expect to like *Star Trek, the Next Generation?* _____
Source: *World Almanac and Book of Facts*

24. In 1800, there were only about 6 people per square mile of land in the U.S. What was the approximate population in 1800 if there were about 364,700 square miles in the U.S.?
Source: *World Almanac and Book of Facts*

Practice 7-4 Problem-Solving Strategy: Solve a Simpler Problem

Solve by using a simpler problem.

1. At 8:00 P.M., there are 243 people in line for a ride at an amusement park. Every 12 minutes starting at 8 P.M., 42 people are able to enter the ride. A boy gets in line at 8:00. Will he get to ride before the ride shuts down at 9:00 P.M.? Explain.

   _____

   _____

2. The astronauts who landed on the moon brought back about 842 pounds of moon rocks. Dividing the cost of these moon flights by the weight of the rocks, it is estimated that the rocks cost $3,000,000 per ounce. What was the approximate cost of these moon flights? _____

3. While an adult is asleep, his or her heart can pump about 80 gal of blood per hour. About how many gallons of blood will the heart pump during a week of sleep if an adult sleeps 7 h each night? _____

Use any strategy to solve each problem. Show all your work.

4. The Language Club includes students who are enrolled in Latin, German, Spanish, or French. Each person, including John, is enrolled in only one foreign language. Christine does not speak French. Judy is enrolled in German or Latin. Pepe is enrolled in Latin or Spanish. Christine and the person taking Spanish often walk to school together. Christine and the person who is taking German are best friends. Who is enrolled in which course?

   _____

   _____

5. What is the sum of all odd numbers from 101 to 200?

   _____

6. A small hummingbird beats its wings 70 times/s. How many times will it beat its wings in 8 h?

   _____

7. It takes the sound of thunder five seconds to travel one mile. How far away is the thunder if it takes 45 s to reach you?

   _____

8. A company with 628 employees is taking all the employees to see a baseball game. The company will hire buses. If each bus holds 34 passengers, will 15 buses be enough? _____

   _____

Practice 7-5 Scale Drawings

For Exercises 1–6, use a ruler and the scale to find the actual length indicated.

1.

1 cm to 2 m

_____

2.

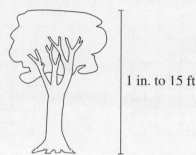

1 in. to 15 ft

_____

3.

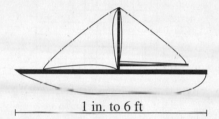

1 in. to 6 ft

_____

4.

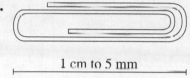

1 cm to 5 mm

_____

5.

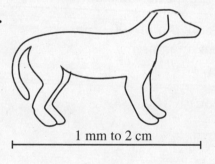

1 mm to 2 cm

_____

6.

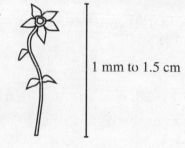

1 mm to 1.5 cm

_____

7. Find the measure in cm of your thumb from the tip of your fingernail to where it meets your wrist. If you drew a $\frac{3}{4}$-size picture of yourself, how long would your thumb be in the drawing? _____

8. The length of a wall in a floor plan is $6\frac{1}{2}$ in. The actual wall is 78 ft long. Find the scale of the floor plan. _____

9. The height of a building is $3\frac{3}{8}$ in. on a scale drawing. Find the actual height of the building if the scale used is

1 in. : 4 ft.

Practice 7-6 Percent Sense Using Models

Use the 10 × 10 square grid to model each percent.

1. 72%

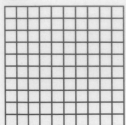

2. 14%

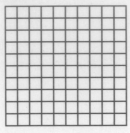

3. 34%

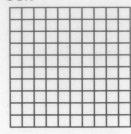

4. 56%

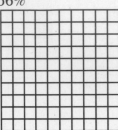

5. 5%

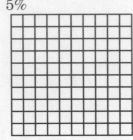

6. 11%

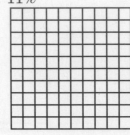

Write each amount as a percent.

7. 37 students out of 100 students have blue eyes. _____

8. 3 lightbulbs per every 100 lightbulbs were found to be defective. _____

9. 92 votes out of 100 votes were "yes." _____

10. 29 students out of 100 students live in an apartment. _____

For Exercises 11–13, use the whole numbers 1 through 100.

11. What percent of the numbers are even numbers? _____

12. What percent of the numbers are multiples of 6? _____

13. What percent of the numbers are multiples of 8? _____

14. A human's brain makes up about 2% of his or her body weight. What is the approximate weight of the brain of a person who weighs 100 lb? _____

15. Approximately 65% of a person's body weight is water. Merga's aunt weighs 100 lb. How many pounds are water? _____

16. Sixteen percent of the seventh-graders at East Side School chose art as an after-school interest. What percent of the students did not choose art? _____

Name _____ Class _____ Date _____

Practice 7-7 *Percents, Fractions, and Decimals*

Write each fraction as a decimal and as a percent.

1. $\frac{3}{5}$ _____ **2.** $\frac{7}{10}$ _____ **3.** $\frac{13}{25}$ _____ **4.** $\frac{17}{20}$ _____

Write each decimal as a percent and as a fraction in simplest form.

5. 0.02 _____ **6.** 0.45 _____ **7.** 0.4 _____ **8.** 0.92 _____

Write each percent as a decimal and as a fraction in simplest form.

9. 46% _____ **10.** 17% _____ **11.** 90% _____ **12.** 5% _____

The table shows the fraction of students who participated in extracurricular activities from 1965 to 1995. Complete the table by writing each fraction as a percent.

Students' Extracurricular Choices

Year	1965	1970	1975	1980	1985	1990	1995
Student participation (fraction)	$\frac{3}{4}$	$\frac{8}{10}$	$\frac{17}{20}$	$\frac{39}{50}$	$\frac{21}{25}$	$\frac{19}{25}$	$\frac{87}{100}$
Student participation (percent)	____	____	____	____	____	____	____

Write each fraction or decimal as a percent. Write the percent (without the percent sign) in the puzzle.

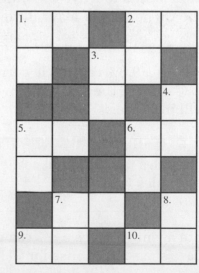

Across

1. $\frac{3}{5}$

2. $\frac{1}{5}$

3. 0.55

5. 0.23

6. $\frac{7}{20}$

7. 0.17

9. 0.4

10. $\frac{9}{25}$

Down

1. $\frac{13}{20}$

2. 0.25

3. $\frac{1}{2}$

4. $\frac{3}{20}$

5. 0.24

6. $\frac{3}{10}$

7. 0.1

8. $\frac{4}{25}$

Course 1 Chapter 7

Practice 7-8 *Estimating with Percents*

Draw a model to help you estimate each amount.

1. 81% of 60 _____

2. 20% of 490 _____

3. 48% of 97 _____

Circle A, B, C, or D. Determine the best estimate.

4. 72% of 80
  A. 64   **B.** 56
  C. 6   **D.** 5.6

5. 18% of 90
  A. 18   **B.** 9
  C. 27   **D.** 1.5

6. 21% of 80
  A. 20   **B.** 160
  C. 16   **D.** 1.6

7. 39% of 200
  A. 80   **B.** 60
  C. 100   **D.** 72

8. 81% of 150
  A. 80   **B.** 120
  C. 160   **D.** 60

9. 68% of 250
  A. 140   **B.** 210
  C. 150   **D.** 175

Solve.

10. Mr. Andropolis wants to leave the waitress a 12% tip. Estimate the tip he should leave if the family's bill is $32.46.

  _____

11. Michael receives a 9.8% raise. He currently earns $1,789.46 per month. Estimate the amount by which his monthly earnings will increase.

  _____

12. Estimate the sales tax and final cost of a book that costs $12.95 with a sales tax of 6%.

  _____

13. A real estate agent receives a 9% commission for every house sold. Suppose she sold a house for $112,000. Estimate her commission. _____

Name _____ Class _____ Date _____

Practice 7-9 *Finding a Percent of a Number*

Find each percent.

1. 15% of 20 _____

2. 40% of 80 _____

3. 20% of 45 _____

4. 18% of 70 _____

5. 90% of 120 _____

6. 65% of 700 _____

7. 25% of 84 _____

8. 63% of 80 _____

9. 60% of 50 _____

10. 45% of 90 _____

11. 12% of 94 _____

12. 15% of 52 _____

13. 37% of 80 _____

14. 25% of 16 _____

15. 63% of 800 _____

16. 72% of 950 _____

17. 55% of 250 _____

18. 18% of 420 _____

19. 33% of 140 _____

20. 53% of 400 _____

Solve each problem.

21. The Badgers won 75% of their 32 games this year. How many games did they win? _____

22. Vivian earned $540 last month. She saved 30% of this money. How much did she save? _____

23. A survey of the students at Lakeside School yielded the results shown below. There are 1,400 students enrolled at Lakeside. Complete the table for the number of students in each activity.

How Lakeside Students Spend Their Time on Saturday

Activity	Percent of Students	Number of Students
Baby-sitting	22%	
Sports	26%	
Job	15%	
At home	10%	
Tutoring	10%	
Other	17%	

Practice 7-10 Data and Circle Graphs

Sketch a circle graph for the percentages given.

1. Ms. Murphy's Class's Favorite Foods

Pizza	Spaghetti	Hamburger
60%	30%	10%

2. Mr. Chung's Class's Favorite Type of Book

Animal	Sports	Adventure	Mystery
20%	25%	10%	45%

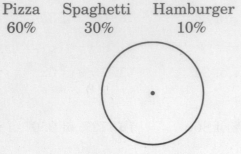

3. Mr. Fano's Class's Favorite Color

Blue	Purple	Red
40%	35%	25%

4. Ms. Ramon's Class's Favorite Sport

Swimming	Softball	Soccer	Hockey
20%	30%	5%	45%

5. Number of TV Stations Received By Homes

1–6	7–10	11–14	15–40	41–60
7%	34%	34%	19%	6%

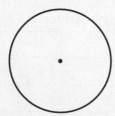

6. Tom Pin's Bowling Record

Games Won	Games Lost	Games Tied	Forfeits
50%	35%	5%	10%

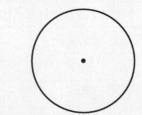

Name _____ Class _____ Date _____

Practice 8-1 Points, Lines, and Planes

Refer to the diagram at the right for Exercises 1–6. Name each of the following.

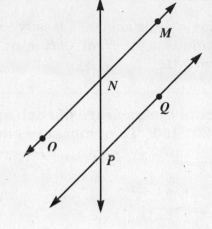

1. three collinear points

   _____

2. three noncollinear points

   _____

3. three segments

   _____

4. three rays

   _____

5. two lines that appear to be parallel

   _____

6. two pairs of intersecting lines

   _____

7. Draw four collinear points.   8. Draw five noncollinear points.

Complete each sentence with *sometimes*, *always*, or *never*.

9. Three points are _____ collinear.

10. Four points are _____ noncollinear.

11. A ray _____ has one endpoint.

12. A line _____ has an endpoint.

Name the segments that appear to be parallel.

13.

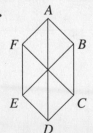

14.

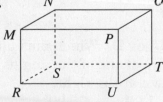

_____   _____

Practice 8-2 Exploring Angles

Use the diagram at the right.

1. Name three rays.

   _____

2. Name three angles. Classify each
   angle as *acute, right, obtuse,* or
   straight.

   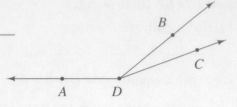

   _____

Estimate the measure of each angle. Choose the best estimate from 30°, 60°, 90°, 120°, 150°. Then measure each angle with a protractor.

3. _____

4. _____

5. _____

6. _____

Use a protractor to draw an angle with each measure.

7. 88°   8. 65°

Use the diagram at the right.

9. Find the measure of ∠*MSN,* ∠*NSO,* ∠*OSP,*
   ∠*PSQ,* and ∠*QSR.*

   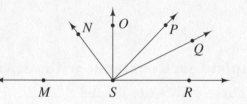

10. List all of the obtuse angles shown.

    _____

11. List all of the right   12. List all the straight   13. List all the acute angles
    angles shown.   angles shown.   shown.

    _____   _____   _____

                                                                _____

                                                                _____

14. **Circle A, B, C, or D.** Which measure
    is not a measure of one of the angles in
    the figure shown at the right?
    A. 45°   **B.** 135°   **C.** 90°   **D.** 120°

    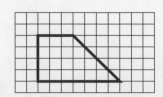

Practice 8-3 Special Pairs of Angles

Complete each sentence with *sometimes, always,* or *never*.

1. Two right angles are _____ complementary.

2. Two acute angles are _____ supplementary.

3. One obtuse angle and one acute angle are _____ supplementary.

4. One obtuse angle and one right angle are _____ supplementary.

Find the measure of each angle marked $x°$.

5.

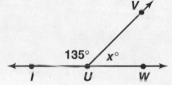

_____

6.

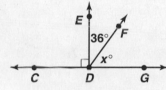

_____

7.

_____

8.

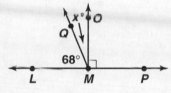

_____

9.

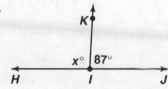

_____

10.

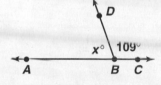

_____

Use the diagram at the right. Name each of the following.

11. two interior angles _____

12. two exterior angles _____

13. two pairs of supplementary angles

_____

14. the transversal _____

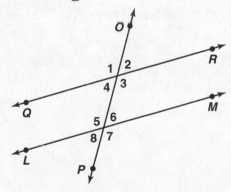

Use the figure at the right to solve.

15. Find the measure of the angle marked $x°$ at the corner of the picture frame.

_____

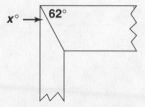

Practice 8-4 Identifying Triangles

Use a centimeter ruler and protractor to measure the
sides and angles of each triangle. Classify each triangle
according to its angle measures and side lengths.

1.

2.

3.

_____ _____ _____

Classify each triangle with given side lengths as
scalene, isosceles, or *equilateral.*

4. 8, 9, 8 _____   **5.** 3, 4, 5 _____
6. 15, 15, 15 _____   **7.** 4, 7, 9 _____

Classify each triangle with given angle measures as
acute, right, or *obtuse.*

8. 60°, 60°, 60°

_____

9. 25°, 14°, 141°

_____

10. 90°, 63°, 27°

_____

11. 90°, 89°, 1°

_____

Sketch each triangle. If you can't sketch a triangle,
explain why.

12. a right obtuse triangle

13. an acute equilateral
triangle

14. an isosceles scalene
triangle

_____ _____ _____
_____ _____ _____
_____ _____ _____
_____ _____ _____

Practice 8-5 Exploring Polygons

Name each polygon.

1. _____   2. _____   3. _____

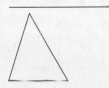   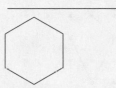   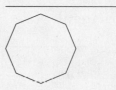

4. _____   5. _____   6. _____

Use the dot paper below to draw each polygon.

7. a quadrilateral with one right angle

8. a pentagon with no right angle

9. a hexagon with two right angles

. . . .
. . . .
. . . .
. . . .
. . . .

10. Trace and cut out the following polygons. Rearrange the polygons to form a lowercase "t".

  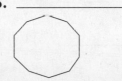

11. Trace the plus sign and cut it into four identical polygons. Rearrange the polygons to form a square that has the same height and width as the plus sign.

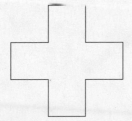

▬▬Practice 8-6 Classifying Quadrilaterals

Use the diagram at right for Exercises 1–14. Identify all the polygons that have each name.

1. quadrilateral

   _____

2. parallelogram

   _____

3. rhombus

   _____

4. rectangle

   _____

5. square

   _____

6. trapezoid

   _____

State the *best* name for each polygon.

7. a   8. b   9. c   10. d

   _____   _____   _____   _____

11. e   12. f   13. g   14. h

   _____   _____   _____   _____

Sketch an example of each quadrilateral.

15. a parallelogram that   16. a quadrilateral that   17. a rectangle
    is not a rectangle   is not a parallelogram

18. How many squares can you find in the figure?

    _____

19. Move four of the line segments from the large square so that three squares result.

Practice 8-11 Slides, Flips, and Turns

Draw two translations of each shape.

1.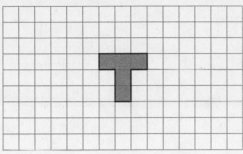

2.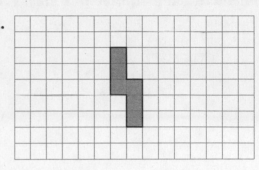

Draw the reflection of each shape. Use the dashed line as the line of reflection.

3.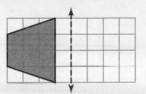

4.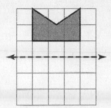

5.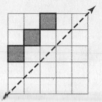

Tell whether each shows a translation or a reflection.

6.

7.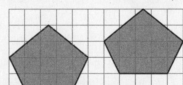

8.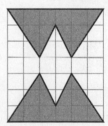

_____   _____   _____

Are the shapes of each of the following rotations the shape at the right? Write *yes* or *no*.

9.

10.

11.

12.

_____   _____   _____   _____

Practice 9-1 Estimating Area

The area of each square is 1 cm². Find the area of each figure.

1.

_____

2.

_____

3.

_____

Each square represents 1 in.². Find the area of each figure.

4.

_____

5.

_____

6.

_____

7. **Circle A, B, C, or D.** Each square represents 100 m².
   Which is the best estimate for the area of the figure?

   A. 250 m²   **B.** 2,500 m²

   C. 2,000 m²   **D.** 1,500 m²

8. Outline the letters of your first name on the graph paper
   below. Make the letters as large as possible. Shade in the
   letters and then find the area. Each square represents
   1 cm².

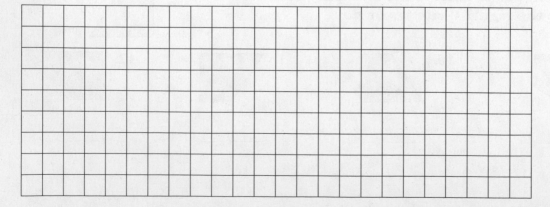

Name _____ Class _____ Date _____

Find the area and perimeter of each rectangle.

1.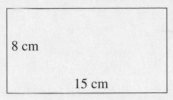
8 cm

15 cm

2.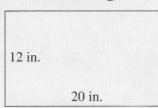
12 in.

20 in.

3.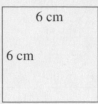
6 cm

6 cm

_____   _____   _____

**Use a centimeter ruler to measure the length and width of
each rectangle. Mark the length and width on each figure.
Then find the perimeter and area.**

4.

5.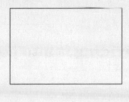

6.

_____   _____   _____

Choose a calculator, paper and pencil, or mental math to solve.

7. The length of a rectangle is 8 cm. The width is 6 cm.

  a. What is the area? _____   **b.** What is the perimeter? _____

8. The area of a rectangle is 45 in.^{2}. One dimension is 5 in. What is
the perimeter? _____

9. The perimeter of a square is 36 cm. What is the area of the
square? _____

10. The perimeter of a rectangle is 38 cm. The length is 7.5 cm. What
is the width? _____

11. The figure at the right contains only squares.
Each side of the shaded square is 1 unit.
What is the length, width, and area of the figure?

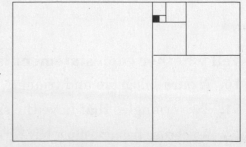

_____

Practice 9-3 Areas of Parallelograms and Triangles

Find the area of each figure.

1.

_____

2.

_____

3.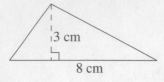

3 cm

8 cm

_____

4.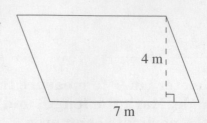

4 m

7 m

_____

Find the area of each figure by dividing it into polygons.

5.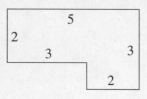

5

2

3   3

2

_____

6.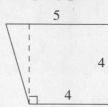

5

4

4

_____

7.

2

4

3   1

_____

8.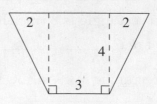

2   2

4

3

_____

9. Draw and label a triangle and a parallelogram that each have an area of 20 square units.

Tell whether each statement is *true* or *false*.

10. A parallelogram and triangle can have the same base and area. _____

11. Two triangles that have the same base always have the same area. _____

12. An obtuse triangle must have greater area than an acute triangle. _____

▬▬▬*Practice 9-4* Gathering Data to Explore Pi

**Use 3 for π to estimate the circumference of a circle
with the given radius or diameter.**

1. $d = 4$ in. _____

2. $d = 8$ cm _____

3. $r = 6$ m _____

4. $r = 10$ ft _____

5. $r = 3$ in. _____

6. $d = 20$ cm _____

**Use a calculator to find the circumference of a circle
with the given radius or diameter. Round to the
nearest unit.**

7. $r = 18$ cm _____

8. $d = 44$ ft _____

9. $r = 28$ in. _____

10. $r = 24$ m _____

11. $d = 34$ in. _____

12. $d = 42$ cm _____

**Use a calculator to find the diameter of a circle with the given
circumference. Round to the nearest unit.**

13. $C = 128$ ft _____

14. $C = 36$ cm _____

15. $C = 200$ m _____

16. $C = 85$ in. _____

17. $C = 57$ cm _____

18. $C = 132$ in. _____

**Complete the table. Use a string and metric ruler to
measure the circumference and the diameter of four
different circular objects. Then check to see if the
ratio $\frac{C}{d} = $ about 3.14.**

Object	Circumference, C	Diameter, d	$\frac{C}{d}$
19.			
20.			
21.			
22.			

23. Use the table you have just completed. What can you
conclude about the ratio $\frac{C}{d}$?

_____

Practice 9-5 Area of a Circle

Use a calculator to find the area of a circle with the given radius or diameter. Round each answer to the nearest tenth.

1. $r = 12$ cm _____

2. $d = 15$ m _____

3. $d = 9$ cm _____

4. $d = 14$ cm _____

5. $r = 22$ m _____

6. $r = 28$ m _____

Use a calculator to find the area of each circle. Round each answer to the nearest tenth.

7.

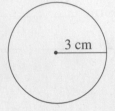

3 cm

_____

8.

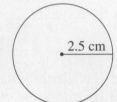

2.5 cm

_____

9.

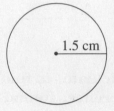

1.5 cm

_____

Use a calculator to find the area of the shaded region. Round to the nearest unit.

10.

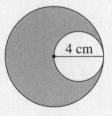

4 cm

_____

11.

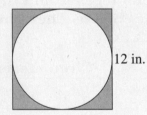

12 in.

_____

Solve each problem. Round to the nearest square inch.

12. Find the area of an 8-in. diameter pizza. _____

13. Find the area of a 12-in. diameter pizza. _____

14. The cost of the 8-in. pizza is $7.00. The cost of the 12-in. pizza is $12.50.

    Which size pizza is the better buy? _____

    Explain. _____

    _____

Practice 9-6 *Three-Dimensional Figures*

Identify each three-dimensional figure.

1.

_____

2.

_____

3.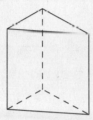

_____

4.

_____

Find the number of faces, edges, and vertices for each figure.

5.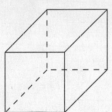

_____

6.

_____

7. Circle A, B, or C. Which of the following is *not* a possible view of a rectangular prism?

A.   **B.**   **C.**

Name the figure you can form from each net.

8.

_____

9.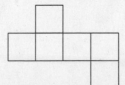

_____

10.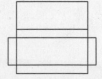

_____

Practice 9-7 Exploring Surface Area

Choose a calculator, paper and pencil, or mental math to find the surface area of the rectangular prism.

1.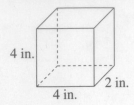

4 in.
4 in.
2 in.

_____

2.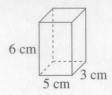

6 cm
5 cm
3 cm

_____

3.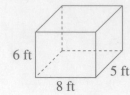

6 ft
8 ft
5 ft

_____

4.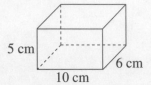

5 cm
10 cm
6 cm

_____

5.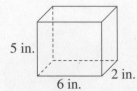

5 in.
6 in.
2 in.

_____

6.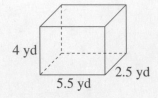

4 yd
5.5 yd
2.5 yd

_____

Find the surface area of the rectangular prism that has the given net.

7.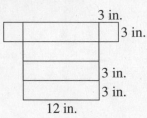

3 in.
3 in.
3 in.
3 in.
12 in.

_____

8.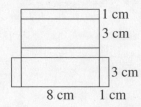

1 cm
3 cm
3 cm
8 cm   1 cm

_____

Draw or build a rectangular tower of centimeter cubes. Make the bottom layer 4 cm by 3 cm, and make 5 layers. Assume that you can view any face of the tower.

9. How many cubes have at least one side visible? _____

10. How many cubes are hidden from view inside the tower? _____

11. What is the surface area of the tower? _____

■■■ *Practice 9-8* *Volume of a Rectangular Prism*

Find the volume of each rectangular prism.

1.

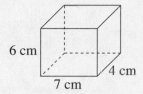

6 cm
7 cm
4 cm

_____

2.

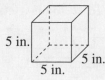

5 in.
5 in.
5 in.

_____

3.

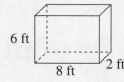

6 ft
8 ft
2 ft

_____

4. $l = 6$ cm, $w = 5$ cm, $h = 12$ cm

_____

5. $l = 13$ in., $w = 7$ in., $h = 9$ in.

_____

**The volume and two dimensions of a rectangular prism
are given. Find the third dimension.**

6. $V = 140$ ft^3, $l = 5$ ft, $h = 7$ ft

_____

7. $V = 255$ cm^3, $w = 17$ cm, $h = 3$ cm

_____

8. $V = 343$ in.^{3}, $h = 7$ in., $l = 7$ in.

_____

9. $V = 280$ yd^3, $l = 14$ yd, $w = 4$ yd

_____

**Draw and label a rectangular prism with the given
volume, using a set of whole-number dimensions.**

10. $V = 90$ cm^3

11. $V = 200$ cm^3

Solve each problem.

12. A fish aquarium measures 3 ft long, 2 ft wide, and 2 ft
high. What is the volume of the aquarium?

_____

13. A swimming pool is 25 ft wide, 60 ft long, and 7 ft deep.
What is the volume of the pool? _____

Practice 9-9 *Problem-Solving Strategy: Make a Model*

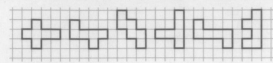

Choose any strategy to solve each problem. Show all your work.

1. Circle the nets that you could fold to form a cube.

2. Find three numbers that continue the pattern.

   1, 3, 7, _____, _____, _____

3. Describe two different ways to continue the pattern.

   2, 3, 5, _____, _____, _____

   2, 3, 5, _____, _____, _____

4. How many different rectangles can you form using 24 centimeter squares?

   _____

5. What is the area of the parallelogram at the right? Assume that each square represents 1 cm².

   _____

6. **Circle A, B, or C.** Which piece of plastic wrap shown below can be used to cover the surface of the box shown? The piece can overlap, but cannot be cut.

   A. 12, 16   **B.** 16, 20   **C.** 12, 12

7. A farmer has 3 sons. The farmer decides to give each son the same amount of seeds and barrels. The farmer has 21 barrels: 7 are full of seeds, 7 are half-full, 7 are empty. You cannot move seeds from one barrel to another. How can the farmer divide the seed and barrels equally? Make a model to help solve.

   _____

   _____

Practice 10-1 Using a Number Line

1. Graph these integers on the number line: –4, 9, 1, –2, 3.

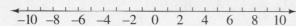

Name the integer that is represented by each point.

2. J _____ **3.** K _____

4. L _____ **5.** M _____

Write an integer to represent each situation.

6. spent $23 _____ **7.** lost 12 yards _____ **8.** deposit of $58 _____

Name the opposite of each integer.

9. 16 _____ **10.** –12 _____ **11.** 100 _____ **12.** 75 _____

Compare. Write <, >, or =.

13. –5 ☐ 8 **14.** 13 ☐ –14 **15.** –11 ☐ –19

Name an integer between the given integers.

16. –2, 9 _____ **17.** 3, –12 _____ **18.** –7, –11 _____

Complete with an integer that makes the statement true.

19. –9 > _____ **20.** _____ > 3 **21.** 0 > _____

22. List the temperatures from least to greatest. _____
   • The temperature was 25°F below zero.
   • The pool temperature was 78°F.
   • Water freezes at 32°F.
   • The low temperature in December is –3°F.
   • The temperature in the refrigerator was 34°F.

Think of the days of a week as integers. Let today be 0, and let days in the past be negative and days in the future be positive.

23. If today is Tuesday, what integer stands for last Sunday? _____

24. If today is Wednesday, what integer stands for next Saturday? _____

25. If today is Friday, what integer stands for last Saturday? _____

26. If today is Monday, what integer stands for next Monday? _____

Practice 10-2 Modeling Integers

Write the integer that is represented by each set of tiles. Unshaded tiles represent positive integers and shaded tiles represent negative integers.

1. _____

2. _____

3. _____

4. _____

5. _____

6. _____

7. _____

8. _____

9. _____

Shade the tiles to represent each integer in two ways. Use unshaded tiles for positive integers and shaded tiles for negative integers.

10. −4
   a. ☐☐☐☐
   b. ☐☐☐☐☐☐
      ☐☐

11. 5
   a. ☐☐☐☐☐
   b. ☐☐☐☐☐☐
      ☐☐☐☐

12. 7
   a. ☐☐☐☐☐☐☐
   b. ☐☐☐☐☐☐☐☐
      ☐

13. −8
   a. ☐☐☐☐☐☐☐☐
   b. ☐☐☐☐☐☐☐☐
      ☐☐☐☐

14. 2
   a. ☐☐
   b. ☐☐☐☐☐
      ☐☐☐☐☐

15. −9
   a. ☐☐☐☐☐☐☐☐☐
   b. ☐☐☐☐☐☐☐
      ☐☐☐☐☐☐

Shade the tiles to represent the given integer.

16. 4
   ☐☐☐☐☐☐☐☐

17. −3
   ☐☐☐☐☐☐☐☐☐☐

18. −6
   ☐☐☐☐☐☐☐☐☐☐☐☐

19. 0
   ☐☐☐☐☐☐☐☐☐☐

20. Draw models of all possible integers that can be represented using 4 tiles.

   ☐☐☐☐   ☐☐☐☐   ☐☐☐☐   ☐☐☐☐   ☐☐☐☐

   _____   _____   _____   _____   _____

Practice 10-3 Modeling Addition of Integers

Write a numerical expression for each model. Find the sum. Unshaded tiles represent positive integers and shaded tiles represent negative integers.

1. _____   **2.** _____   **3.** _____

Choose paper and pencil or mental math to find each sum.

4. −2 + (−8) _____   **5.** 8 + (−4) _____   **6.** −6 + 3 _____

7. 6 + (−4) _____   **8.** −1 + 7 _____   **9.** −8 + 3 _____

10. −2 + (−6) _____   **11.** 6 + (−9) _____   **12.** −5 + (−7) _____

13. −4 + (−7) _____   **14.** 4 + (−7) _____   **15.** −4 + 7 _____

Compare. Write <, >, or =.

16. −5 + (−6) ☐ 6 + (−5)   **17.** −8 + 10 ☐ −3 + 6

18. 4 + (−9) ☐ −8 + (−5)   **19.** 20 + (−12) ☐ −12 + (−4)

Solve.

20. Bill has overdrawn his account by $15. There is a $10 service charge for an overdrawn account. If he deposits $60, what is his new balance? _____

21. Jody deposited $65 into her savings account. The next day, she withdrew $24. How much of her deposit remains in the account? _____

22. The outside temperature at noon was 9°F. The temperature dropped 15 degrees during the afternoon. What was the new temperature? _____

23. The temperature was 10° below zero and dropped 24 degrees. What is the new temperature? _____

24. The high school football team lost 4 yd on one play and gained 9 yd on the next play. What is the total change in yards? _____

25. Philip earned $5 for shoveling snow, $2 for running errands, and received $8 allowance. He spent $6 at the movies and $3 for baseball cards. How much money does he have left?

_____

Course 1 Chapter 10

Practice 10-4 Modeling Subtraction of Integers

Write a numerical expression for each model. Find the difference.

1.  _____

2. 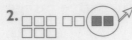 _____

3.  _____

4. _____

Choose paper and pencil or mental math to find each difference.

5. $2 - 5$ _____   **6.** $-5 - 2$ _____   **7.** $-6 - 3$ _____

8. $10 - (-3)$ _____   **9.** $-9 - (-2)$ _____   **10.** $0 - (-5)$ _____

11. $-12 - (-3)$ _____   **12.** $8 - 13$ _____   **13.** $11 - (-6)$ _____

Compare. Write <, >, or =.

14. $5 - 12 \ \square\ 5 - (-12)$ **15.** $8 - (-5) \ \square\ -8 - 5$

16. $9 - (-4) \ \square\ 4 - (-9)$ **17.** $-12 - 12 \ \square\ 12 - (-12)$

Solve each equation.

18. $t + 15 = 10$ **19.** $8 + c = 3$ **20.** $x - 12 = -3$ **21.** $s + 6 = 1$

_____   _____   _____   _____

Solve.

22. The temperature was 48°F and dropped 15° in two hours. What was the temperature after the change? _____

23. The temperature at midnight is –5°C and is expected to drop 12° by sunrise. What is the expected temperature at sunrise? _____

24. Catherine has $400 in her checking account. Her utility bills total $600. How much more money does she need to pay the utility bills? _____

25. On the first play, the football team lost 6 yd. On the second play, the team lost 5 yd. What was their total change in yards? _____

26. Use the thermometer to find the final reading at 1 P.M. _____

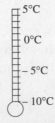

10 A.M.	reading of 5°C
11 A.M.	drops 5°C
12 noon	drops 3°C
1 P.M.	drops 4°C

Practice 10-5 Problem-Solving Strategy: Use Multiple Strategies

Use one or more strategies to solve each problem. Show all your work.

1. The stick-on digits 0, 1, 2, 3, 4, 5, 6, 7, 8, and 9 can be bought at hardware stores. You need to label 100 lockers from 1 to 100 with the stick-on digits. Which digit will be used the least number of times? the most? _____

2. A commuter train passes through the station every half hour from 6 A.M. through 7 P.M. How many trains pass through the station each day? _____

3. Marika is older than Will and younger than Jean. Marika is younger than Kisha. Jean is older than Ty and younger than Megan. Ty is older than Marika. Who is the youngest? _____

4. Seven schools will play each of the other schools once in a soccer tournament. How many games need to be played?

_____

5. Arrange the digits 0, 1, 2, 3, 4, 5, 6, 7, 8, and 9 to form two five-digit numbers so that the difference is as large as possible.

6. Weekend admission charges at the zoo are $3.50 for adults, $1.50 for seniors, and $2.00 for children (5–12 years old). Children under 5 are admitted free. The parking fee is $3.00. What is the total cost for a group of four adults, two seniors, and children with ages 3, 4, 5, 6, 7, 8, 9, 10, 11, and 12 that came in three cars? _____

7. Al went shopping and spent half his money and $5 more at a gift shop. At the food store, he spent half his remaining money and $5 more. He had only $2.50 left. How much money did Al have when he went into the gift shop?

_____

8. The last Friday of last month was the 26th day of the month. What day of the week was the first day of last month?

_____

9. How many calls will be made among six people if each person needs to talk to each of the other people one time?

_____

Practice 10-6 Graphing Functions

Complete each function table.

1. Input	Output
1	5
2	10
3	15
4	___
5	___

2. Input	Output
10	20
20	40
30	60
40	___
50	___

3. Input	Output
3	6
4	7
5	8
6	___
7	___

Make a function table for each function.

4. ounces as a function of pounds

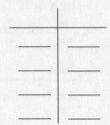

5. pints as a function of cups

6. yards as a function of inches

Graph each function.

7. Hours	Wages ($)
1	15
2	30
3	45
4	60

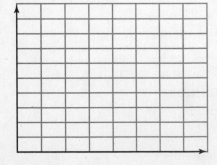

8. Gallons	Quarts
1	4
2	8
3	12
4	16

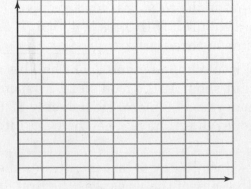

9. Use your graphs from Exercises 7–8.
   a. Find the wages for 6 hours. _____
   b. Find the number of quarts for 7 gallons. _____

Practice 10-7 Graphing on the Coordinate Plane

Name the point with the given coordinates.

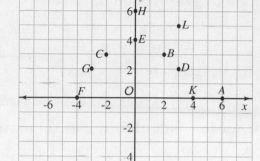

1. (2, 3) _____   2. (−4, 0) _____

3. (−3, −5) _____   4. (0, 6) _____

5. (3, 5) _____   6. (4, 0) _____

Write the coordinates of each point.

7. J _____   8. E _____

9. D _____   10. A _____

11. G _____   12. C _____

Identify the quadrant in which each point lies.

13. (8, −4) _____   14. (−4, 8) _____   15. (4, 8) _____

16. (−8, −4) _____   17. (8, 4) _____   18. (−4, −8) _____

Use the coordinate plane below.

19. Graph four points on the coordinate plane so that when the points are
   connected in order, the shape is a rectangle. List the coordinates of the points.

   _____

20. Graph four points on the coordinate plane so that when the points are
   connected in order, the shape is a parallelogram that is not a rectangle. List the
   coordinates of the points.

   _____

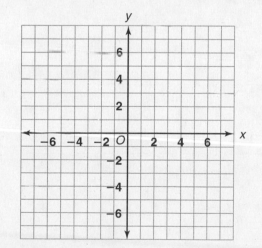

Practice 10-8 Applying Integers and Graphs

What scale and intervals would you use on the vertical axis to graph each data set?

1. 5, –9, 18, –6, 12, 16   _____

2. –13, 8, –10, 5, 9, 2   _____

3. –45, 40, –16, –8, –26, 32   _____

4. –10, –26, 18, 11, 3, –2   _____

Choose a calculator, mental math, or paper and pencil.

5. –18 + 7 _____   6. 16 – 37 _____   7. 326 + (–326) _____

8. 43 – (–18) _____   9. 1,258 + (–271) _____   10. –73 + (–92) _____

11. Find the closing balance for each day.

Day	Expenses	Income	Balance
Sunday	–$32	$45	
Monday	–$40	$50	
Tuesday	–$26	$40	
Wednesday	–$50	$45	
Thursday	–$35	$30	
Friday	–$70	$60	
Saturday	–$53	$60	

12. Draw a line graph to display the balances in Exercise 11.

13. On which day did the greatest balance occur? _____

14. On which day did the least balance occur? _____

15. What was the total balance for the week? Was it a loss or profit?

_____

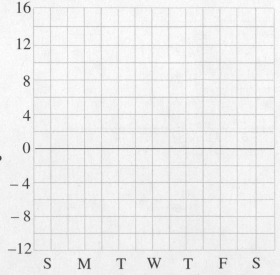

Practice 11-1 Fair and Unfair Games

Mirga and José played a game and completed the table below.

Mirga wins	𝈫𝈫𝈫𝈫𝈫𝈫𝈫𝈫𝈫𝈫 I
José wins	𝈫𝈫 I
Times played	𝈫𝈫𝈫𝈫𝈫𝈫𝈫𝈫𝈫𝈫𝈫𝈫 II

1. Find Probability(Mirga wins) and Probability(José wins).

   _____

2. Do you think the game is fair? Explain.

   _____

   _____

Andy and Bryan are playing a game in which Andy wins if the sum of the numbers on 2 number cubes is even, and Bryan wins if the sum of the numbers is odd.

3. Complete the grid at the right.

4. What sum appears most often?

   _____

5. How many outcomes are even numbers?

   _____

6. How many outcomes are odd numbers?

   _____

+	1	2	3	4	5	6
1						
2						
3						
4						
5						
6						

7. Is the game they are playing fair or unfair? _____

8. Nick and Pat are playing a game with a black and white spinner like the one at the right. Nick wins if the spinner stops on black, and Pat wins if it stops on white. Is the game fair or unfair? Explain.

   _____

9. Draw two spinners. Make and label one fair and the other unfair.

▬▬▬ *Practice 11-2* Problem-Solving Strategy: Simulate a Problem

Simulate and solve each problem. Show all your work.

1. Marty makes 60% of his free throws.
    a. What is the probability that he will make two free throws in a row? Draw a spinner to represent his free throw percent. Use the circle at the right. _____
    _____

    b. Marty practices and can now make 80% of his free throws. Draw a spinner to represent his free throw percent. Use the circle at the right.

    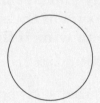

2. Mail is delivered between 12:00 P.M. and 1:00 P.M. every day to Joe's house. Joe comes home for lunch at 11:30 A.M. for 45 min. What is the probability that the mail will arrive during Joe's lunch break? Draw a spinner to represent the times that the mail is delivered. _____

Use any strategy to solve each problem. Show all your work.

3. You have several coins that total 38 cents. You have the same number of pennies as nickels. How many coins do you have?

    _____

A group of 50 middle school students were surveyed about their after school activities. There were 33 students who take dance lessons, 31 students who take music lessons, and 31 students who play organized sports. There are 11 students who do all three activities. Of these 50 students, 5 students only take dance and play sports, 6 students only take music and and play sports, and 12 students only take dance and music.

4. How many take only dance lessons? _____

5. How many take only music lessons? _____

6. How many only play sports? _____

7. There were 10 people at a party. At the end of the party, each person shook hands with each of the others. How many hand shakes were there in all?

    _____

Practice 11-3 Simulations and Random Numbers

Use this list of random numbers for Exercises 1–4 to simulate tosses of two number cubes.

62 31 32 64 55 43 63 11 41 34 24 51 14 15 26 32 22 41 26 31
23 41 63 24 11 25 34 52 22 51 42 63 52 32 43 41 11 24 12 33

1. Are you more likely to get two different digits or the same two digits?

   _____

2. Find the number of pairs with different digits.

   _____

3. Find the number of times the cubes were tossed.

   _____

4. Find Probability(different digits).

   _____

5. Complete the table. Show the possible two-digit numbers formed when two number cubes are tossed.

	1	2	3	4	5	6
1						
2						
3						
4						
5						
6						

6. How many numbers with two different digits were possible in Exercise 5? _____

7. How many possible numbers are there? _____

8. Find Probability (numbers with different digits) as a percent.

   _____

Use this list of random numbers for Exercise 9.

1 1 2 1 1 1 2 1 2 1 1 1 1 2 2 2 1 1 1 1 2 2 1 2 2
1 2 2 2 1 1 1 1 1 2 1 1 2 2 1 2 1 1 2 2 2 2 1 1 2
2 2 2 2 2 2 1 1 1 1 1 1 2 1 2 2 1 2 2 1 1 2 1 2 1

9. Suppose 1 represents a coin toss landing heads. How many times would a coin land heads in the first 50 trials?

   _____

Practice 11-4 *Theoretical Probability*

A number cube is rolled once. Find each probability. Write as a fraction, decimal, and percent.

1. Probability(even) _____

2. Probability(*not* 3) _____

3. Probability(1, 3, or 5) _____

4. Probability(0) _____

5. Probability(1 or 6) _____

6. Probability(less than 7) _____

Use the spinner at the right.

7. Find Probability(white) as a fraction, decimal, and percent.

   _____

8. Find Probability(shaded) as a fraction, decimal, and percent.

   _____

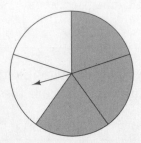

The fund-raising committee sold 500 raffle tickets. Tyrone bought three tickets. There will be one winning ticket.

9. What is the probability that Tyrone will win? _____

10. What is the probability that Tyrone will not win?

    _____

A box contains blue marbles and yellow marbles. One marble is to be drawn. Probability(yellow) = $\frac{5}{12}$.

11. What is Probability(blue)? _____

12. **Choose A, B, or C.** Which spinner could you use to simulate the problem? _____

   A. 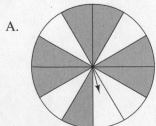   B. 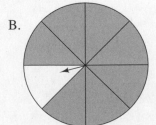   C.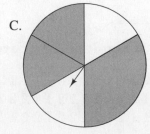

13. If the box contains 24 marbles, how many of each color are there?

    _____

Practice 11-5 Tree Diagrams and the Counting Principle

Each shape in a set of attribute blocks comes in two sizes (small and large), three colors (yellow, red, and blue), and two thicknesses (thick and thin).

1. Use a tree diagram and list all the different blocks for each shape.

2. How many outcomes are possible?

   _____

3. Find Probability(red)

   _____

4. How many outcomes will be blue and thin? _____

5. How many outcomes will be large? _____

6. Show how you could use the counting principle to find the number of outcomes. _____

7. Suppose a medium size is also available. What is the new total outcomes? _____

Each day Jake makes his lunch for school. Today he can choose from white, rye, or wheat bread. He can choose turkey, cheese, or ham slices.

8. Draw a tree diagram to show all possible sandwiches.

9. How many sandwich choices would he have if lettuce were an option? _____

Marguerite has socks in 4 different colors (red, blue, white, and black) and shoes in 3 different colors (blue, white, and black).

10. What is the probability that she will choose white socks and white shoes? _____

11. What is the probability that she will choose matching socks and shoes? _____

◼◼◼Practice 11-6 *Independent Events*

Use the spinner at the right for Exercises 1–5. It is spun twice.

1. Use multiplication to find the probability that the first spin is white and the second spin is black. _____

2. Draw a tree diagram to show all possible outcomes.

3. Find the probability that the two spins are different colors. _____

4. Find the probability that the two spins are the same color. _____

5. Are the spins independent events? Explain
_____

6. Assume a number cube is rolled. Find Probability(4). _____

7. The number cube is rolled again. Find Probability(4). _____

8. Find the probability of rolling 5 two times in a row. _____

9. Find the probability of rolling two 4's in a row. _____

A coin is tossed four times.

10. Find Probability(HTHT). _____

Suppose each letter of your name is printed on a separate card.

11. One card is drawn from a container holding first-name letters. Find Probability(first letter of your first name).

_____

12. One card is drawn from a container holding last-name letters. Find Probability(first letter of your last name).

_____

13. One card is drawn from each container. Find Probability(your initials).

_____

Practice 11-7 Exploring Arrangements

1. Make an organized list of how Ali, Ben, and Chou can sit in a row one behind another.

2. Make an organized list of all possible arrangements of the letters in the word BITE. How many of the arrangements are English words? _____

3. Mrs. Schoup has three errands to do on her way home from work.

   a. Draw a tree diagram to show all the different arrangements of going to the post office, the library, and the gas station.

   b. How many different ways can Ms. Schoup organize her errands? _____

4. Vince has homework in math, science, language, and reading. How many different ways can he do his homework?

   _____

5. The spring program will feature songs from five grade levels. How many different ways can these grade levels be arranged?

   _____

6. How many different ways can six posters be displayed side-by-side? _____

7. Amy can scramble the letters in her name and make two more words. How many different ways can the letters in her name be scrambled into nonwords? _____

8. How many different ways can you scramble the letters in your first name? _____

Use a calculator to find each value.

9. 6!   10. 9!   11. 5! + 5   12. 11!

_____   _____   _____   _____

Practice 11-8 Making Predictions from Data

Answer each question in a complete sentence in your own words.

1. What is a population? _____

   _____

   _____

2. What is a sample? _____

   _____

   _____

3. When is a sample random? _____

   _____

   _____

4. Why must a sample be representative of the whole population?

   _____

   _____

For Exercises 5–7, state whether the sample is random. Explain.

5. To provide better service to the town, the library plans to increase its hours of operation. For a two-week period, it is surveying each patron who checks out books.

   _____

   _____

   _____

6. A permanent traffic signal is being considered at a certain intersection. An electronic counter records the times and numbers of vehicles from 6:00 A.M. to 9:00 P.M. for one week.

   _____

   _____

   _____

7. A book publisher wants to know the opinions of 12-year-olds in a school district. The name of each 12-year-old is placed in a bin and 20 names are chosen.

   _____

   _____

   _____

Enrichment: Minds on Math

For Lessons 1-1 through 1-3

1-1

Each member of a team wears a T-shirt with a different consecutive number starting with one. The team members work in 6 pairs on a warm-up exercise. The sum of the numbers on the T-shirts of every pair of students is the same. Reynold is wearing a T-shirt with the number 5 on it. What is the number on his partner's T-shirt?

1-2

I am a 2-digit number. The difference between the product of me and myself and the sum of me and myself is 99. What number am I?

1-3

Two dogs stood on a hill. The little dog was the big dog's son, but the big dog wasn't the little dog's father. How is this possible?

Course 1 Chapter 1

Enrichment: Minds on Math

1-4

I am a 3-digit palindrome. I do not change when my digits are reversed. My first digit is twice my middle digit. The sum of my digits is 10. What palindrome am I?

1-5

Draw the figure shown below without lifting your pencil from the paper and without retracing any line.

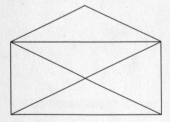

Enrichment: Minds on Math

1-6

How many 4-digit numbers can you make using the digits 1, 4, 6, and 9 if you use each digit only once in each number?

1-7

Perry said he is thinking of a number that is as much greater than 36 as it is less than 94. What is Perry's number?

Course 1 Chapter 1

Enrichment: Minds on Math

2-1

Draw as many different lines as possible that pass through any two of the points below. How many different lines are possible?

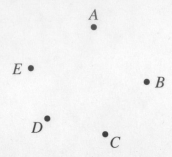

2-2

Look at the keypad of a telephone. Of the ten keys that show the digits 0 to 9 (ignore the * and # keys), there are different sets of four keys that are at the corners of squares. For only one such set do the digits have an odd sum. What is that sum?

2-3

Write the letters A, B, C, D, and E in the squares so that the same letter is not used more than once in any row, column, or diagonal.

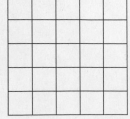

Enrichment: Minds on Math

2-4

The number on Julie's softball jacket has 2 digits. Her number is a multiple of 3, 4, 5, and 6. What is Julie's number?

2-5

Find the missing digits in the number below if the number is the product of two equal factors.

2,☐ ☐ 5

Enrichment: Minds on Math

2-6

How many different rectangles can you find in the figure below?

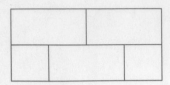

2-7

What single-digit numbers do ◯, ☐, and △ represent in the expressions below?

$$☐ - △ = 3$$

$$◯ \times △ = 30$$

$$◯ + △ + ☐ = 20$$

▬▬▬Enrichment: Minds on Math

3-1

Jeremi, Orin, and Marcia all like yogurt. They all like a different flavor best. Their favorites are vanilla, lemon, and strawberry. Jeremi's favorite is not vanilla. Orin likes strawberry best. What flavor does Marcia like best?

3-2

I am a three-digit number. My last digit is three times my first digit. My first digit is twice my middle digit. What number am I?

3-3

During a pancake eating contest Team A ate 8 more pancakes than Team B. Team C ate twice as many pancakes as Team B. Together, the three teams ate a total of 72 pancakes. How many pancakes did Team A eat?

■■■ Enrichment: Minds on Math

3-4

At Monroe Middle School there are 79 students in three sixth-grade history classes. The classes are different sizes. The largest class has 28 students. How many students are in the smallest possible class?

3-5

Write the numbers 0 through 5 in the circles, using five digits only once and one digit twice, so that the numbers in any three circles connected by a straight line total 10.

3-6

Danielle thinks of two numbers that are multiples of 9. The product of the two digits (neither a 9) of either of her numbers is also a multiple of 9. What are her numbers?

Enrichment: Minds on Math

For Lessons 3-7 through 3-10

3-7

Six days after the day before yesterday is Monday. What
day is it today?

3-8

Hayley is 2 in. taller than Vi. Tina is 5 in. shorter than Alli.
Alli is 1 in. shorter than Hayley. Who is the shortest?

3-9

I am a two-digit number less than 100. When I am divided
by 2, 3, 4, or 5, the remainder is 1. What number am I?

3-10

Draw 3 lines without lifting your pencil to divide the
square into 4 identical triangles.

Enrichment: Minds on Math

4-1

How many different three-digit numbers can be formed using the digits 1, 4, and 9 only once in each number?

4-2

Four boxes of baseball trading cards had the same number in each box. Andrew, Andrea, and Amy divided the trading cards evenly. If they each got 48 cards, how many trading cards were in each box?

4-3

Change two operations in the expression below to make the value of the expression equal to 35.

$5 + 5 + 5 + 5 + 5 + 5$

Enrichment: Minds on Math
For Lessons 4-4 through 4-6

4-4

What single-digit numbers do □ and △ represent in the equation below?

$$(□ + △) \times (□ + △ + □) = 88$$

4-5

I am a four-digit number. All of my digits are different. My first digit is twice my fourth digit. My second digit is twice my first digit. My last digit is twice my third digit. The sum of my digits is 15. What number am I?

4-6

Margaret, Ron, and Eugene each bought a new movie. They each chose a different type of movie: science fiction, musical, or romance. Ron never watches science fiction. Margaret watches only musicals. What type of movie did each person buy?

Enrichment: Minds on Math
For Lessons 4-7 through 4-10

4-7

Rebecca's little sister Tina has 48 yellow blocks and 40 green blocks. Tina builds some number of towers using all 88 blocks. What is the greatest number of identical towers that Tina can build?

4-8

Write the numbers 1 through 9 in the circles, using each digit only once, so that the numbers along each side of the triangle have a sum of 20.

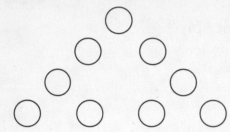

4-9

Karl keeps losing buttons. One minute after losing one button, he lost another. He lost another button two minutes later, and then he lost another button four minutes later, and so on. Will Karl lose 25 buttons in one year?

4-10

Gerri told Paul that if she began with 15, multiplied by 3, divided by some number, and then added 10, the result would be 15. By what number did Gerri divide?

Enrichment: Minds on Math

For Lessons 5-1 through 5-3

5-1

Which 4 sides of the small squares would you remove to leave 5 small congruent squares?

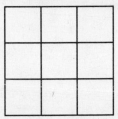

5-2

Norma used a total of 192 digits to number the pages of her book. How many pages are there in Norma's book?

5-3

Suppose you have 2 quarters, 5 dimes, and 10 nickels. How many ways can you make change for 50¢?

Enrichment: Minds on Math   *For Lessons 5-4 through 5-6*

5-4

Lilli and Micah are in line at a movie theater. There are 2 people in line between them. There are twice as many people in front of Lilli as there are in front of Micah. How many people are in line in front of Lilli?

5-5

How many different triangles can you find in the figure below?

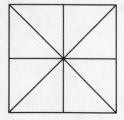

5-6

Use only 5s and plus signs to fill in the ten boxes to get the sum shown. ☐☐☐☐☐☐☐☐☐☐ = 1,165

Enrichment: Minds on Math
For Lessons 5-7 through 5-10

5-7

Kilta's house number has 4 different digits. The sum of the last two digits is 6 greater than the sum of the first two digits. The number is a multiple of 5. The first digit minus the second digit is 1. The last digit minus the first digit is 4. What is Kilta's house number?

5-8

Fill in the boxes with the numbers 1 through 9 so that the sum of the numbers in each indicated row, column, and diagonal is 15.

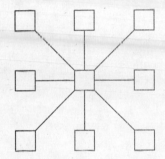

5-9

What single-digit numbers do □ and △ each represent in the expressions below?

$$\square + \square = \triangle \times \triangle$$

$$\square + \square + \square + \square = \square \times \triangle$$

5-10

Ira has 4 lengths of chain with 3 links each. He wants to join the 4 lengths to form one circular chain with 12 links. How can he do this if he cuts and rejoins only 3 links?

Enrichment: Minds on Math   For Lessons 6-1 through 6-3

6-1

Fill in each ☐ with one of the digits 4, 5, 6, 7, 8, or 9 to find the least possible difference. Use each digit only once.

6-2

Margaret and Jimmy are playing a game called 99 to 100. They start with 99 and add or subtract certain numbers until they reach 100. The object is to be the first player to get to 100. Margaret and Jimmy decided that they would only be allowed to add 11 or subtract 7 on each move. What is the fewest number of moves that can be made before someone wins the game?

6-3

How can you cut a board with dimensions 8 ft by 3 ft to cover a hole with dimensions 12 ft by 2 ft if you can only make one cut in the board?

Enrichment: Minds on Math

6-4

One of 27 marbles weighs less than the other 26 marbles which are of equal weight. What is the least number of weighings on a balance scale needed to determine the odd marble?

6-5

A group of 32 students was sitting in a row of chairs. They began with 1 and counted off by 1s. Each student who counted a multiple of 2 stood up. Then only the students who were still sitting counted off by 1s. Again, each student who counted a multiple of 2 stood up. They kept repeating this procedure. How many times will they need to do this before only one student is sitting?

6-6

Turn the triangle of circles "upside down" by sliding one circle at a time to a new location so that it touches 2 other circles. The minimum number of moves is 3.

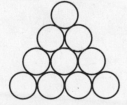

Enrichment: Minds on Math

For Lessons 6-7 through 6-10

6-7

Rio's grandfather is 2 times as old as Rio's dad. Twenty years ago the ratio of their ages was 3 to 1. How old is Rio's grandfather now?

6-8

Suppose that every 15 min a cell divides into 2 cells. If there were 4,000 cells at 12:00 p.m., at what time were there 500 cells?

6-9

I am a proper fraction in simplest form. My numerator is a two-digit prime number. My denominator is 4 more than my numerator. Three of my digits are the same and are also a prime number. What fraction am I?

6-10

How many different rectangles can you find in the figure below?

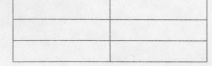

Enrichment: Minds on Math

7-1

How can you cut a bagel into eight equal pieces with just 3 cuts?

7-2

Damian and Heather ran home from school. Damian ran half the distance and then walked the rest of the way. Heather ran half the time and then walked the rest of the time. If they both ran at the same speed and walked at the same speed, who got home first? Explain your answer.

7-3

Mr. Addis makes some shelves with 3 pegs and some with 4 pegs. Yesterday he used 24 pegs to make some shelves of each type. How many of each type of shelf did he make?

Enrichment: Minds on Math

7-4

I am a two-digit prime number. The number formed by reversing my digits is also prime. My ones digit is 4 less than my tens digit. What number am I?

7-5

Replace 5 of the digits with zeroes in the problem below so the remaining numbers will have a sum of 1,111.

```
    111
    333
    777
 +  999
```

7-6

Jason is cutting 50-ft coils of wire into 6-ft pieces. Each of his 5 workers needs 6 of these pieces. How many full coils does Jason need?

■ Enrichment: Minds on Math
For Lessons 7-7 through 7-10

7-7

Rachel is thinking of a three-digit number. She tells Steven that when she divides her number by the sum of the digits of her number, the quotient is 26. She tells him that her number is the least one for which this is true. What is Rachel's number?

7-8

I am the least number that has factors of 1, 2, 3, 4, 5, 6, 7, and 8. What number am I?

7-9

A restaurant supplier sells plastic forks in packages of 30 and plastic knives in packages of 24. Micah wants to buy the same number of forks and knives. What is the minimum number of packages of each he would have to buy?

7-10

Eve sold candles to raise money for her school. After the first day, she sold 3 more candles than the day before for 6 days. If she sold 24 candles on the last day, how many candles did she sell on the first day?

▬▬ Enrichment: Minds on Math

8-1

I am the least three-digit number that is divisible by 22 and the sum of whose ones digit and tens digit is 11. What number am I?

8-2

Find the missing numbers if each number after the first two is the sum of the two preceding numbers.

____, 8, ____, ____, ____, 56.5

8-3

A number has 4 digits.
The sum of the first digit and the last digit is twice the second digit.
The second digit is 2 less than the third digit.
The last digit is twice the first digit.
Some of the digits are alike.
What is the number?

▰▰▰ Enrichment: Minds on Math

8-4

Nathan is weighing blocks and balls. Each of the blocks weighs the same and each of the balls weighs the same. The weight of 4 blocks and 1 ball is the same as the weight of 2 blocks and 2 balls. Which is heavier: a block or a ball? How much heavier?

8-5

Which six sides of the small squares would you remove to leave 2 squares?

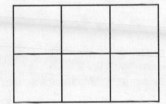

8-6

Fred said to Tara, "Give me eight books and we'll have an equal number." Tara answered, "If you give me eight books, then I will have twice as many as you." If both Fred and Tara are correct, how many books did each have?

8-7

Marcus makes three flower arrangements in four hours. At this rate, how long will it take him to make five flower arrangements?

Course 1 Chapter 8

Enrichment: Minds on Math

For Lessons 8-8 through 8-11

8-8

I am a fraction in simplest form. One-sixth of me is the same as one-half of one-fourth. What fraction am I?

8-9

I am a quadrilateral with one obtuse angle, one acute angle, and two right angles that share one of my sides. What kind of quadrilateral am I?

8-10

I am a polygon that can be called a rectangle or a rhombus. What polygon am I?

8-11

How many parallelograms can you find in the figure below?

◼◼◼◼ *Enrichment: Minds on Math*   **For Lessons 9-1 through 9-3**

9-1

In September, $\frac{1}{2}$ of the customers at Tommy's Discount Store paid for their purchases by check. Of the remaining customers, $\frac{2}{3}$ paid with a credit card and the rest paid cash. What fraction of the customers paid cash?

9-2

I am a percent that is less than 100%. As a decimal I can be written with one digit to the right of the decimal point. When I am written as a fraction in simplest form, the numerator and denominator are single digits and their difference is 3. What percent am I?

9-3

Items at a garage sale were priced at $1, $2, and $5. Marty spent $21. He bought one more item for $2 than items for $1. He bought twice as many $2 items as $5 items. How many of each item did he buy?

▬ Enrichment: Minds on Math

9-4

The diameter of a circle is tripled. How does this affect the area of the circle?

9-5

The figure below has an area of 180 in.^{2} and consists of 5 congruent squares. How can you rearrange the squares to make a figure with a perimeter of 60 in.?

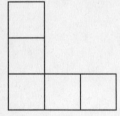

9-6

Heather folded a square sheet of paper in half. Then she cut the sheet of paper along the fold. She told Wayne that the perimeter of each of the rectangles formed was 18 in. What was the area of Heather's original square sheet of paper?

■■■ Enrichment: Minds on Math *For Lessons 9-7 through 9-9*

9-7

Terri's cube has a surface area of 6 cm^2. Each edge of
Quinn's cube is twice as long as each edge of Terri's cube.
What is the surface area of Quinn's cube?

9-8

A rectangular pool has dimensions of 20 ft by 30 ft. There
is a walkway that is 8 ft wide surrounding the pool. Find
the area of the walkway.

9-9

I am a rectangle. My perimeter is 26 in. and my area is
36 in.^{2}. What are my dimensions?

Enrichment: Minds on Math   *For Lessons 10-1 through 10-3*

10-1

Henry, Curtis, and Crista guessed the number of buttons in a jar. Henry guessed 113 buttons, Curtis guessed 119 buttons, and Crista guessed 120 buttons. One of the guesses was correct, one missed by 6, and one missed by 1. Who guessed the correct number of buttons?

10-2

I am a four-digit multiple of 9. My first two digits are the same and my last two digits are 58. What number am I?

10-3

Change one of the operational symbols in the expression below so that the value of the expression is multiplied by 4.

$81 - 12 - 13 - 14 - 15 - 17$

◼️◼️ Enrichment: Minds on Math   *For Lessons 10-4 through 10-6*

10-4

Tomorrow will not be Monday or Friday. Today is not Tuesday or Wednesday. Yesterday was not Thursday or Sunday. What day was yesterday?

10-5

Mrs. Brown, Mrs. Black, and Mrs. Green have brown, black, and green raincoats. "None of our coats matches our names," says Mrs. Green. "You're right!" says the lady in the brown coat. Who has which coat?

10-6

I am a fraction. My numerator is 3 less than my denominator. My reciprocal is 4 times my value. What fraction am I?

Enrichment: Minds on Math

10-7

Margie made corn muffins. Her family ate $\frac{1}{3}$ of them. She then gave $\frac{1}{4}$ of the remaining muffins to her neighbors and put the rest in the freezer. If she put 9 muffins in the freezer, how many muffins did she make?

10-8

Jordan bought a CD for $5. He sold it for $10, and then bought it back for $15. Finally, he sold it for $20. Did Jordan make money, lose money, or break even? If he made money or lost money, how much did he make or lose?

Enrichment: Minds on Math
For Lessons 11-1 through 11-3

11-1

Write the numbers 1 through 12 in the magic star, using each number only once, so that the sum of numbers at the six points of the star and in each of the six rows is 26.

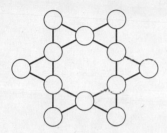

11-2

How many squares are in a 5 by 5 square grid?

11-3

The ratio of females to males in the computer club is 6 to 5. If four females and six males miss a meeting, the ratio is 10 to 7. How many students are in the computer club?

Enrichment: Minds on Math

For Lessons 11-4 through 11-6

11-4

Karol is decorating a cube with 7 colors of paint. She paints 2 dots of each color on each side of the cube. How many dots does she paint on the cube?

11-5

Find the next four numbers in the pattern.

$-1, 2, -2, 1, -3,$ ___, ___, ___, ___

11-6

I am an integer. When you add -1 to me, the sum is the opposite of the difference when you subtract -5 from me. What integer am I?

▄▄▄▄ *Enrichment: Minds on Math*   *For Lessons 11-7 through 11-8*

11-7

In a barnyard full of cows and chickens, there are 30 more legs than heads. If the ratio of cows to chickens is 4 to 3, how many cows are in the barnyard?

11-8

Someone once said "Sisters and brothers have I none, but that man's father is my father's son." Explain how this can be true.